GARETH BENSON, LLB

IDEAOLOGY

Your Compass to Intellectual Property Success in the Ideas Economy

First published by Gareth Benson Enterprises Pty Ltd ACN 650 960 768 2021

First edition

ISBN: 978-0-6452128-3-9

Editing by Léandre Larouche
Proofreading by Aris Kalamaras

This book was professionally typeset on Reedsy.
Find out more at reedsy.com

To all the innovators, creators and history shakers.
Thank you for your thoughts.

Contents

Welcome to the Ideas Economy

S omewhere off the Australian coast, a hundred years ago, two brothers working as pearl divers contemplated their future. They were working harder than ever, yet they were making less money than before. The struggles of World War I in Australia were fresh in their minds, and between the rising cost of living and inflation, they saw their income diminish and their quality of life suffer.

The two pearl divers worked on a pearl lugger for long hours six days a week. They were paid decently for the pearls they found, but that didn't afford them the freedom to live and spend time with their family. Many of their relatives lived thousands of miles away on a Greek island dreaming of a better life. The pearl divers had a few weeks off work every year, but they never had time to return home. Every year, they communicated with their relatives via letters, which would take months to arrive. They were grateful for a new life in Australia, but in reality, they were enslaved to their job.

The brothers had two problems. One problem was they were enslaved to their job. The other problem was that their work was dangerous. The brothers had to dive deep into the sea and could get stung by all kinds of sea creatures, not to mention the risk of running out of oxygen. The pearl divers didn't hate their job, though. It was a part of their identity. They loved the craft they had perfected. In fact, they had developed rare expertise. But despite the beauty of diving in remote parts of Australia and their love for the work, the two brothers found themselves unfulfilled.

They didn't know how, but they knew something had to change.

One day, out of fatigue and frustration, the two brothers decided they had had enough. They would no longer work on someone else's ship; rather, they would invest in their own ideas and become the captain of their own ship. They had one quest, one mission: to find Australia's best mother of pearls. By now, it had become evident to the two brothers they would not accomplish this mission on somebody else's ship.

The two brothers moved to Darwin, Australia, where they began their own enterprise. They bought their first lugger, then their second and then their third. They began hiring people and gave them meaningful work. At that point, the northern Australian coast was one of the world's most generous pearling ports. Sailing off the world's demand, and armed with a bold, entrepreneurial mindset, they embarked on a promising enterprise. But as they would soon find out, one does not become an entrepreneur for comfort or security.

The following years were years of struggle and adaptation. Not only did the First World War disrupt markets and the way of life, but the 1950s also witnessed a dramatic decrease in demand for pearls. As if this weren't enough, frequent cyclones and other adverse weather made pearl diving difficult and threatened the brothers' ships. The brothers, however, did not so easily give up. Instead, they partnered with Japanese experts and revolutionised the pearl industry. Today, the brothers' family name is associated with a legacy of entrepreneurship and innovation. The brothers not only succeeded in their pearl diving enterprise, but they also built a billion-dollar business empire.

Fast forward three decades and this Australian family perfected the process to harvest some of the most beautiful pearls on the planet. They redefined the industry and their pearls are still a sought-after luxury item. Today, they remain the most well-regarded producer of cultured pearls. Most importantly, these unlikely entrepreneurs went from sailors to captains of their own ship and found that their processes could employ others to farm fresh pearls in some of the most remote regions of Australia. Crucially, they went from divers, doing the hard and dangerous work themselves, to captains of their own idea. They also became one of the most successful Greek entrepreneur families in Australia.

If you have picked up this book, you likely have an entrepreneurial idea. Perhaps it's the spark of an idea ready to combust into action, or perhaps it's simply the desire to fan your own flames of success. Perhaps you dream of great wealth, or perhaps you wish to follow your purpose. The good news is that the story I have just recounted is one from the past century. Since then, things have changed—and a lot. There has never been a greater time than today to bring your ideas into the

3

world. The past 60,000 years of known human civilisation have witnessed vast technological progress. In the last 400 years alone, we've seen more significant advancements in creativity, science and technology. Today more than ever before, you can become the captain of your ideas and set sail towards a blue ocean of success.

If you look deep enough inside yourself, you will see you have the skills, knowledge and expertise to sail through uncharted waters and find the treasure you seek. There are many new frontiers still to be discovered and many rewards to be found. But to become the captain of your idea, you must learn how to commercialise it and bring it to market. This starts with intellectual property. I wrote this book to give you a clear compass to navigate this process whether you are thinking about an entrepreneurial idea or already are a business owner. There are many books on business, entrepreneurship, marketing and intellectual property. But you need to understand how these different fields converge. As an intellectual property lawyer and consultant, this is my specialty.

To give you a bit more context, I was born into a family of educators, academics and businesspeople who valued new ideas. My grandfather was an engineer in the Indian Railway Company. In India, he met my grandmother, an Australian nurse, and they gave birth to my father shortly after. Our other relatives were tea traders who had come to India to capitalise on this opportunity. My family's greatest legacy, however, isn't a business. It is the foundation of a few schools where, still to this day, people in India are taught to read and write. I draw a lot of inspiration from my family's legacy, and the fact that I live in the greatest age of opportunities makes me even more awestruck.

What inspires me the most about my family is that, despite their great endeavours, they were constrained by the limited technological landscape of the early 20th century. It's hard for us to imagine what it was like to do business and provide education back in those days. Sure, the Industrial Revolution in its time had provided a better quality of life in the 18th and the 19th centuries. Still, the technological landscape was nowhere near what it is today. In the last hundred years, aviation has lifted us to new heights, the supply lines of industry have scaled to global reach, and the digital world has connected and transformed business distribution channels in just 20 years. The escalation of change is grand and is destined to continue.

Today, the technology train is moving faster than ever. This technological train is not only faster, but it's also more accessible. The innovation of yesterday was reserved for those who could financially afford to innovate and take great risks. Today, however, it has never been easier to begin a business with free digital tools. We can create web pages to sell products or services within minutes, we can deliver these products or services through digital platforms and we can use social media to advertise what we offer with the click of a mouse. Moreover, one single idea, if commercialised correctly, can create exponential progress and wealth, and indeed change the world.

Mark Getty, the grandson of a U.S. Billionaire oil tycoon, famously said, 'Intellectual Property is the oil of the 21st century.' 'Look at the richest men a hundred years ago,' he added, 'They all made their money extracting natural resources or moving them around. All today's richest men have made their money out of Intellectual Property'.[i]

We now live in the Ideas Economy, the new Industrial Revolution. Much like the Industrial Revolution of the 18th and 19th centuries, we are witnessing accelerating growth in various industries. We are also seeing a change in how we produce value. The first industrial revolution used water and steam power, the second used power to create mass production and the third uses technology to connect us to a global marketplace. Make no mistake, the way we are producing value is changing. The cogs of industry are now being fuelled by our number-one asset: intellectual property.

The Ideas Economy is your greatest opportunity for success because it allows anyone to create new solutions and scale value like it has never been possible before. But there is one downfall: If left unprotected, ideas can easily be stolen or replicated. Unprotected ideas may be easily stolen and they undervalue work. That said, the law does serve to protect idea makers, creators and history shakers. You may be familiar with 'copyright'. Copyright was created to allow writers to protect their works and obtain a pecuniary or financial benefit from their labour. Today, any product or service needs to be protected and secured with intellectual property to be successful. Ideas alone don't have value; the unique expression of an idea does.

Whether you knew it or not, today presents an incredible opportunity for you as an aspiring entrepreneur, creator or producer. You can become the captain of your idea and sail it to commercial success. And this book will give you a simple framework—the Ideaology compass—to become this captain.

This book will give you a simple framework to thrive in the Ideas Economy. It outlines the five steps to commercialising your ideas by creating intellectual property, the most valuable resource for a successful business plan in the twenty-first century. However, before introducing you to the Ideaology compass, you need to understand the context of this fourth industrial revolution we are well entrenched in.

Talking about industrial revolutions

There have been three industrial revolutions in recent history, and every one of them brought great benefits to societies. For example, when James Watt's steam engine propelled us from the age of agriculture into our industrialised global economy, the social landscape changed greatly. According to some economists, the Industrial Revolution improved the standard of living for the general population and caused a consistent population increase. But there were also detractors and opponents to these great technological changes.[ii]

Some pages of the book of history focus on the dirty and dangerous factories in which people worked. Other pages note the towering progress made in health, literacy and social mobility. The net benefit of the Industrial Revolution was no doubt positive, but the disruption to the economy caused uncertainty. Some people resisted the change, some welcomed it and some were forced into it. Still, what is abundantly clear is that those who saw the tides of change rise (and prepared to see the blue sky of opportunities) were then able to ride the wave. Those who didn't were greatest opp—history does not remember them.

The Industrial Revolution reduced the barriers between city and country people. It enabled access to education, housing and infrastructure in cities. To a large degree, it expanded the wealth of the middle class. A lifeline of opportunity and a road out of poverty came into existence. The Industrial Revolution also saw the dilution of class barriers. With the advent of capitalism as we know it today, the rigid constraints keeping citizens from moving from one class to the other shattered before the anguished eyes of an outdated aristocracy. It no longer mattered which family, city or university one came from. Everybody could create and embrace opportunity as they saw fit.

It is how we react to revolutions before us that informs our capacity for success. One of the important distribution channels of the last century, the production line, was created and leveraged by entrepreneurs such as Henry Ford and Thomas Edison. But this era is coming to an end; the gears of the machine that has for so long propelled our economy are about to break. We have already entered the digital revolution.

Today we sit on the cusp of this revolution. In a matter of decades, *Amazon* went from a humble online bookshop to a business colossus, revolutionising industries with its click-and-collect product delivery models. We have seen the world truly embrace the technological revolution presented to us with the birth of the internet. We have begun working from home, embraced digital technologies and moved to more regional areas. The shift in how we live our lives and conduct business, which started in the 1990s, has only accelerated and is nowhere near slowing down.

The end of the production line?

The production line, and by implication the supply chain, influenced the way we think about business and, to some degree, our education system. Many corporations still organise themselves into silos of functions that create value along a 'value chain,' known otherwise as departments. The education and university system has organised itself to follow suit. In fact, the offering for yesterday's university students has always been academic disciplines that offer skills and research in terms of 'departments.' Universities, in this sense, also reflect the factory silos of a distant past.

Educational institutions all over the world have taught students 'skills,' but they haven't taught them to solve problems, let alone to understand human purpose. Whether it be finance, science, medicine, law or business, the education system has provided the labour market with skills to service the production line. The digital revolution, however, has eroded this model which led to a point of distribution only known for twenty or so years. Today, with cloud computing, software-as-a-service and mobile communication tools, businesses can grow and distribute value in the most immediate supply chain ever known to man—the internet.

The digital world will continue to transform the way we think, trust and do business, much like James Watt's steam engine changed everything during the Industrial Revolution. Most important of all, the students of tomorrow will build and leverage their ideas to solve the problems of tomorrow. However, this must start with an acknowledgement that the world has changed, and we need to act differently than we have before. We need to understand that intellectual property stands at the core of everything we do. But in this process, we will inevitably come across 'Luddites,' who attempt to stop or slow down progress. You may even be tempted to be one.

Beware of Luddites

The Luddites were textile workers and self-employed weavers who, in 19th-century England, feared the end of their trade. They protested labour-economising technologies primarily developed between 1811 and 1816. The stocking frames, spinning frames and looms introduced during the Industrial Revolution threatened to replace them with less-skilled, less-paid labourers and leave them without work. The Luddites ultimately caused a region-wide rebellion in Northwestern England, which required a massive deployment of military forces to suppress. The problem with Luddites is that they tried to halt inevitable progress and focused their energy on protest instead of improvement.

Today, the word 'Luddite' is synonymous with a refusal to advance. Though the Luddites resisted change, they were ultimately proved wrong, and we now remember them as standing on the wrong side of history. It's important to embrace the changes before us and to see the opportunities that engulf the market. There is incredible wealth and purpose to be found in this process. Furthermore, the world will change whether we want it or not. If you want to prosper in this new economy, you can't afford to be a Luddite. Nor can you afford to listen to the Luddites, who, if you allow them, will try to dismantle the machinery of your success.

Enter the Matrix

At the turn of this century, as I was finishing law school at Monash University in Melbourne, Australia, a science-fiction film left its mark on the world's psyche. Amongst the news of a 'dotcom' boom and anxiety about the millennium bug (apparently sent to fry our clocks at midnight on January 1, 2000), the Wachowski sisters created a mythology for our modern-day era not seen since *Star Wars*. In my first legal role as a commercial intellectual property lawyer, I worked on the Village Roadshow distribution deal around the *Matrix* sequels. Looking back now, *The Matrix* was a story that propelled me to new frontiers.

The Matrix begins with Neo sitting by his computer searching for something. At best, he is lacklustre about his day job as a software programmer. At worst, he is about to get fired because he is spending all night surfing the internet. He is searching for something—meaning, perhaps. 'It's the question that drives us,' says Trinity, a renowned hacker whom Neo finds after going down the rabbit hole of the existential dread that inhabits him. By the end of the film, Neo finds a new, exciting life waiting for him. This is the invitation in front of us, if we find the courage to pursue it. Apart from precursing the modern information age, *The Matrix* also has the appeal of a powerful modern-day

11

mythology for this new industrial revolution.

Today's possibilities are great and the profits real. There is one condition, however, to be a part of this Ideas Economy: You must embrace our entrepreneurial identity. As in *The Matrix*, you must choose between the 'blue pill' and the 'red pill.' You can either choose a comfortable, painless existence or you can choose an exciting life of creation and growth. If you wish to become the captain of your idea and build a prosperous business, you know which pill to take.

This book is called *Ideaology* and, as I'm sure you noticed, it is a play on the word 'ideology'. As an intellectual property lawyer, I am in a constant dialogue with idea makers, creators and entrepreneurs across the globe. In other words, I work with ideas and the humans that drive them. They are idea makers, creators and history makers, and I stand with them.

I am a strong believer in this new industrial revolution and its potential to improve the world in which we live. I also believe in the level of human consciousness and self-realisation required to take an idea to market. Some may object to my enthusiasm, but what I propose is without a doubt a positive ideology, rich in abundance, that we should embrace for success and finding our own gold.

This book is a call to take advantage of this revolution. It is an invitation to become the captain of your idea, or what I call becoming an 'Ideaologist'.

Think about it: 400 years ago, the agricultural revolution gave farmers, fisheries and foresters new tools to embrace prosperity. 150 years ago, people's prospects could be greatly improved by moving from the country to the city to join factories that boomed during the advent of the production line. Today, however, we need only enter the matrix and ride the entrepreneurial wave to create greater opportunities, which are more easily accessed. When we are truly ready to embrace this change, we can harness the power of our ideas and sail towards new blue oceans of success.

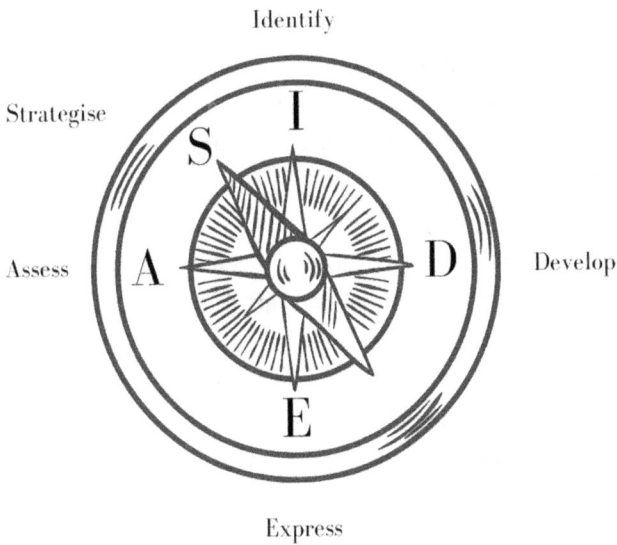

Identify

Strategise

Assess

Develop

Express

The Ideaology Compass

To become the captain of your idea and find your treasure, you must go on a journey that requires interpersonal growth. You need not only to build your ship and gather a crew, but also to find the hero within yourself, which will give you the strength and courage to become the captain of your idea. The Ideaology compass provides you with a tried-and-proven tool to assist you in navigating and successfully sailing your idea across the globe.

1. Identify your idea

Before you can build a product or service, you need to focus on the creation of a powerful idea. For an idea to be worthwhile, it needs to solve a problem. And to find a problem you can solve, you need to look deep within yourself.

What problem do you personally seek to solve in the world? This question is a great place to start. If connected to a sense of purpose, the problem you seek to solve will fuel your research. This question contains not only the intellectual property you need for success but also the power to fuel your engine of opportunity. In 'Identify', you will learn how to look for ideas within yourself and how to combust them into action.

2. Develop your idea

Once you've found your idea, namely, your problem and your solution, you need to build it into something tangible. By tangible, I do not necessarily mean something physical. Remember that many of this era's products and services are digital. Google, Facebook and Canva are all cloud-based businesses and have billions of dollars of intangible assets. To create valuable assets, you need to have a story, or what we shall call 'heroic currency'.

We make sense of the world through stories, and it is critically important to develop our ideas into a cohesive narrative. To do so, you will need to stay firm on your vision and the problem you seek to solve in the world. In 'Develop', you will learn how to craft a compelling narrative for your idea and give it heroic currency to draw a team, opportunities and resources to your venture.

3. Express your idea

In today's economy, ideas can escalate to scalable businesses in just a few years. These ideas can be anything from a software platform to an online gift shop to a publishing business. These businesses can scale to the height of billion-dollar unicorns that service the world even from Australia (think of Atlassian, Red Balloon and Canva, for example).

But to be scalable and attract capital, ideas need to be protected through intellectual property. You wouldn't jump out of a plane without a parachute, so why would you go into business without protecting your ideas? The expression of ideas is more valuable than ideas themselves. Intellectual property creates tangible, protectable assets out of your ideas. In 'Express', you will learn which types of protection exist and which ones you should use for your specific idea.

4. Assess your idea (through valuation)

What's it all worth? Once you have intellectual property assets, you need to value the precious cargo. An often-neglected step in the commercialisation process is the valuation of intellectual property. The days of valuing a business purely on its physical assets are over. Learning to value the intangible value of your business will ensure that you have not only protected your assets, but that you have also leveraged them for financial gains. It will ensure that, when the time is right, an investor will pay the right price for shares of your business. In 'Assess', you will learn how to value your non-physical assets, which will help you accelerate your growth.

5. Strategise and commercialise your idea

Once you have a properly expressed and valued idea, you need a strategy to bring it to market. Although the most important, this step in the entrepreneurial journey is also the least understood. It consists in creating an actual plan to reach the market with your idea and intellectual property. There are several tools you can use to leverage your enterprise in an innovation economy, and you are only confined by the limits of your imagination. Successful commercialisation requires sound and decisive strategy. In 'Strategise', you will learn the different tools and strategies you can use.

Altogether, the Ideaology compass will show you the way to creating great intellectual property assets you can use to drive progress in the world and live the purpose you seek.

Get set to sail and become the captain of your idea, an Ideaologist.

Gareth Benson, LLB.

References

[i] *The Economist*, 'Blood and Oil.' [website], https://www.economist.com/business/2000/03/02/blood-and-oil, (accessed August 1, 2021).

[ii] Nardinelli, Clark, 'Industrial Revolution and the Standard of Living.' *The Library of Economics and Liberty.* https://www.econlib.org/library/Enc/IndustrialRevolutionandtheStandardofLiving.html, (accessed August 1, 2021).

POINT 1: IDENTIFY YOUR IDEA

'The greatest gift we can give is ourselves.' –Joseph Campbell

Before you can build a product or service, you need a compelling idea. For an idea to be worthwhile, it needs to solve a problem. To find a problem you can solve, you need to look within yourself. This first point on the Ideaology compass is designed to help you identify your idea by delving deep into your identity. By the end of this chapter, you will have a clear picture of what your entrepreneurial idea is.

What problem do you personally seek to solve in the world? This question is a great place to start. If connected to a sense of purpose, the answer, with time, will become obvious to you. This question contains not only the intellectual property you need for success, but also the power to fuel your engine of opportunity. There are four steps to identifying your idea:

- Know yourself
- Use design thinking
- Mind map your idea
- Start with a story

Before we go over these tools, however, we need to cover what intellectual property is and the relationship between entrepreneurship and ideas.

Intellectual property is the creation of value

Intellectual property (IP) is just like any other type of property (e.g., real estate). The difference between IP and other property types is that, for centuries, it hasn't been considered tangible. Perhaps that is why business owners often miss it. Intellectual property is the fruit of human intellect, and in the age of ideas, one of the world's most valuable assets. The reason IP is so valuable is that it protects your ideas. Before you build your idea, it is important to reflect on whether your business, project or enterprise adds enough value by solving a complex problem. Such research always begins in your own backyard. You need to self reflect and explore how your identity birthed your idea:

- Where, how and why did you encounter the problem you are trying to solve?
- Who are the people that will benefit from your idea, and why do you care about them?
- What about your idea excites you and makes you feel that you can contribute to the world?
- What are the main themes that underlie your ideas, and what do you like about these themes?
- How can this idea make the world better after it's commercialised, i.e., to take it to a market where people will purchase your valuable idea?

SELF   IDEA   PROBLEM
                TO SOLVE

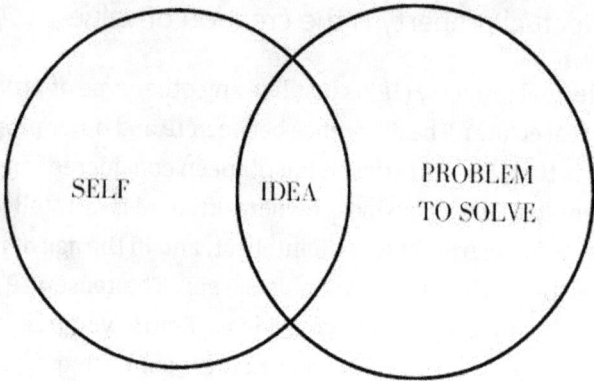

Once you've determined which problem you want to solve, you need to find how you can solve it in an original way. While a faster, better or cheaper product can bring returns in the short term, competing against other products and services on these aspects may not be a long-term strategy. This is the difference between a red ocean and a blue ocean, as Chan Kim and Renée Mauborgne identified in their 2004 book *Blue Ocean Strategy*. A 'blue ocean strategy is the simultaneous pursuit of differentiation and low cost to open up a new market space and create new demand. It is about creating and capturing uncontested market space, thereby making the competition irrelevant. It is based on the view that market boundaries and industry structure are not a given and can be reconstructed by the actions and beliefs of industry players.'[i]

What drives value is innovation, and innovation is the process by which new ideas come to the world. It's important to understand that it's hard to come up with a truly original idea. Most 'new' ideas are, in fact, variations of other ideas that solve an already existing problem.

Just consider the race between Google and Yahoo in the early days of the internet. Both competed to be the number one search engine in the world through speed and result accuracy. Ultimately, Google won this race not simply because it was better, but because it was simple and flexible. Google's code, design and algorithm, i.e., their intellectual property, made the difference between rising to global dominance versus crashing into oblivion as Yahoo did.[ii]

Google and Yahoo were fiercely competitive, but one only needs to look at their landing pages twenty years ago. One solved the problem with a formula to be the fastest search engine and solve the problem of generating the most accurate results. The other was confusing and hard to navigate and ultimately lost its way as they raced. The problem was to assist users find solutions, not to distract and confuse them in their journey search. Problem solvers are always ultimately rewarded based on how easy it is to use their products.

From there, Google's intellectual property has developed in leaps and bounds and is still the company's most valuable asset today.

Entrepreneurship and the value of ideas

Just what is entrepreneurship? Simply put, entrepreneurship is the process of creating something new and useful. It consists of building a system for the market to access our intellectual property, which is the outward expression of our identity. Then, by protecting, valuing and leveraging intellectual property, we can successfully commercialise our ideas, cause progress and generate wealth.

A great example of entrepreneurship is Janine Allis, who, as a young mother, created Boost Juice to make an impact on her children's health. Allis started her company from her home in the early 2000s and then opened her first store in Adelaide, Australia. After seeing some success selling fruit juice and smoothies, she expanded her business activities through franchising. Today, we find Boost Juice locations all over the world, from Asia to Europe, to South America to the United Kingdom. What started as a family business became a global empire. What made it possible? The intellectual property behind Boost Juice, which allowed for franchising.

Another great example of entrepreneurship is Sir Richard Branson, the irreverent British serial entrepreneur. Branson created an empire by treating business as a personal adventure and by making it fun. With the Virgin Group, Branson has ventured in just about every industry you can imagine, and he's also built one of the most valuable brands in the world. Branson doesn't reinvent the wheel with every venture; rather, he puts his own spin on already existing solutions. Branson is living proof that intellectual property is the silent partner to entrepreneurial success.

Steve Jobs, one of the most iconic business leaders of our times, sought to enable others to revolt against the *status quo*. He empowered artists, creators and intellectuals to develop their ideas through personal computers. Through the 1980s and 1990s, Apple and Microsoft, both leaders in personal computing, were fiercely competitive. These two companies weren't just competing for market shares in the personal computer industry; they also fought over intellectual property, which is their most important business asset.

When we search our identity for our ideas, we get closer to making an impact. Problems can be solved in a variety of ways, but only with purpose can they spread like wildfire and reach millions, if not billions, of people. Entrepreneurship creates new value, but the best ideas come from our identity—and it is where we must turn. Identity is how we connect human beings together. Ask yourself who you are, what you care about, and which problem you want to solve, and soon enough, you will find yourself on the path of creating valuable intellectual property.

'Know Thyself'

The most important tenet of the Ideaology approach is that you must know yourself. To build a ship and gather a crew that gets you to your destination, you need to be conscious of who you are and what you stand for. If you work for a start-up or a small-to-medium enterprise, this knowledge may represent

23

your brand identity and your organisation's culture. But this begs the question: How do you find this abundant well and draw up the ideas, which are rich sources of wealth?

Over 2000 years ago, in Delphi, Ancient Greece, seven sages, philosophers, statesmen and lawgivers gathered to inscribe 'know thyself' at the entrance of the Temple of Apollo. For those who travelled on a pilgrimage every year to the mountains of Delphi, the journey was a time of reflection and lead them to the base of this magnificent and magical place. Once they arrived at the base of the mountain, they would lay an offering at the Temple of Apollo. The temple, named after Apollo, the god of music, harmony, light, healing and oracles, was a necessary stop before ascending the mountain, where an Athenaeum was the scene of sports carnivals and feasts of celebration.

This notion of 'knowing oneself' gave a strong sense of identity to the ancient Greeks. To this day, this expression still is a touchstone for Western philosophers; it is, too, an important reminder for us.

Beyond the mere expression it birthed, however, the story of Delphi is an important one. While they went through their pilgrimage, the most important and influential people of Greece took time to reflect, contemplate and create. While at the Temple of Apollo, they served an offering. In other words, they paid tribute to and cared about the creative process.

The story of Delphi is an important reminder for you to take the time to reflect, contemplate and create. While you don't need to undertake a pilgrimage, you should take reflection as seriously as the Greeks did. By doing so, you will not only learn to know yourself—the most important step in the ideation process—but you will also begin generating ideas which can stand the test of time. Early in your entrepreneurial journey, you should dedicate thinking and creative time to help you come up with the ideas that will lead you to success.

Good ideas become great through challenges and interrogation. Socrates, the wise Greek philosopher and one of the world's greatest teachers, used Athens as his classroom, often hosting his dialogues with enthusiastic countrymen to discuss contemporary and philosophical issues. His primary tactic was to ask the question 'Why?' Socratic questioning fundamentally influenced Western thought and underpins the very education system that exists in our country today. To understand ourselves, others and the world around us, we need to ask why things are the way they are. With our changing times, the process of knowing oneself and the world is even more important today. This practice of self-knowledge can be used to foster our sense of purpose and come up with valuable ideas that will change the world. It is also where intellectual property lies, namely, in the unique expression of ideas that solve problems in the world.

If you doubt the path before you, always look for your common purpose in the things that bring you freedom. This will ensure that you are aligned with seeking a treasure that lies within you. When we help others with our gift, we can amplify our freedom.

The Enneagram

There are several tools you can use to explore your identity. The first of these tools is the Enneagram, a system to understand and describe how people interact with the world. The origins of Enneagram models date far back in history and are a matter of dispute. Yet the Enneagram remains to this day a useful tool to connect our ideas with our identity. The Enneagram can be used to understand how we think. I remember first using this tool as a legal specialist for the Commonwealth Scientific and Industrial Research Organisation (CSIRO). The training we undertook revealed to me the importance of knowing how we think. While there is a myriad of self-help books on thinking, I have found the Enneagram to be the most accurate model. Once we understand who we are and how we think, we can proceed to generate ideas that will prove valuable.

According to the Enneagram Institute[iii], there are 9 main Enneagram types:

1. **The Reformer**: The Rational, Idealistic Type: Principled, Purposeful, Self-Controlled and Perfectionistic

2. **The Helper:** The Caring, Interpersonal Type: Demonstrative, Generous, People-Pleasing, and Possessive

3. **The Achiever**: The Success-Oriented, Pragmatic Type: Adaptive, Excelling, Driven and Image-Conscious

4. **The Individualist:** The Sensitive, Withdrawn Type: Expressive, Dramatic, Self-Absorbed and Temperamental

5. **The Investigator:** The Intense, Cerebral Type: Perceptive, Innovative, Secretive and Isolated

6. **The Loyalist:** The Committed, Security-Oriented Type: Engaging, Responsible, Anxious and Suspicious

7. **The Enthusiast:** The Busy, Fun-Loving Type: Spontaneous, Versatile, Distractible and Scattered

8. **The Challenger:** The Powerful, Dominating Type: Self-Confident, Decisive, Willful and Confrontational

9. **The Peacemaker:** The Easygoing, Self-Effacing Type: Receptive, Reassuring, Agreeable and Complacent

THE
PEACEMAKER
9

THE
REFORMER
1

THE
CHALLENGER
8

THE
ENTHUSIAST
7

THE
HELPER
2

THE
LOYALIST
6

THE
ACHIEVER
3

THE
INVESTIGATOR
5

THE
INDIVIDUALIST
4

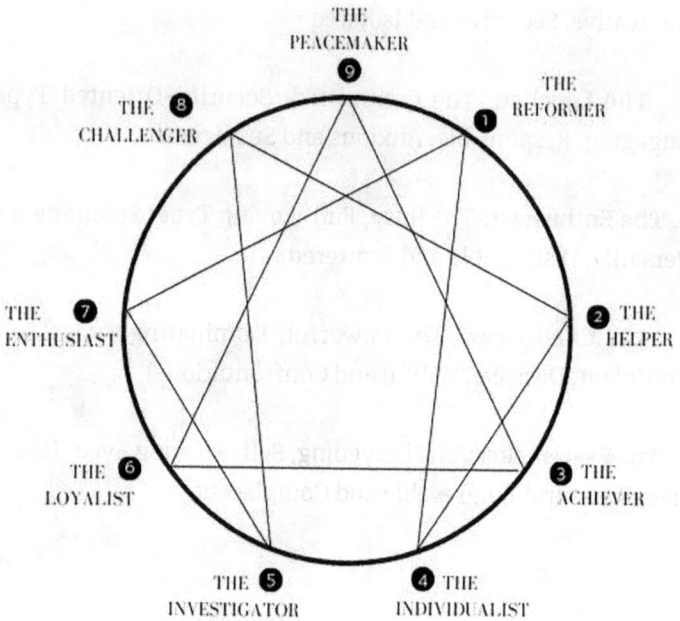

Once you understand who you are and how you think, you can turn to the type of problem you should be working on. This can lead you to the idea that you wish to serve the world. You can also think about the kinds of solutions you can bring to the problem based on your temperament. For example, if you are a Reformer, like Steve Jobs, you might want to tackle problems where you can use your creativity to solve age-old problems. If you're a Helper, like Janine Allis, you might want to think about how you can serve the largest number of people at once through franchising. If you're an Achiever, like Sir Richard Branson, you might want to think about multiplying your ventures and building an empire. Your Enneagram type tells you something about who you are, and who you are tells you something about the type of idea and business you should operate. This will, in turn, generate valuable intellectual property.

After using the Enneagram to determine who you are and which types of ideas make sense for you, you need to start designing your idea. Designing your idea means conceptualising it for the end user. To this end, design and creative thinking are two great tools you can use. It isn't enough to understand yourself and extract your ideas from your identity. You need to meticulously craft an experience for the person meant to use your idea, whichever form your idea may take.

The art of invention: design and creative thinking

Design thinking is a recent trend linked to the articulation and expression of ideas. It employs tools from the world of design while focusing on human behaviour. It is a process by which we design different products or solutions with the user in mind. Design thinking starts by examining the human need for our product or service, which should be easy if we've designed our idea with a problem in mind. Design thinking then focuses on how the user is going to use the service or product. While design thinking does not replace technical skills and technical knowledge, it is a critical tool for the identification and early development of your ideas.

Design thinking unfolds in three parts. First, you must start by forming a few theories about what customers may want but don't have. Second, you must observe their behaviours and look for their journey to the solution. Third, you must test out your idea by using products and services and conducting experiments to see how consumers respond. Finally, you must bring the product to life based on the customers' preferences and commit to a time, location, promotion, and price. Using imaginative, human-focused problem-solving and keeping the customer and the end in mind helps orient the research and development process. While ideation consists of generating ideas, research consists of expanding these ideas and grounding them in reality. Research is how we move from ideas to action. The most important part of this process is to explore the problem by using a range of different tools, including human-centred design thinking.

At the end of the day, human-centred thinking is the diamond set in the centre of entrepreneurship. The way to begin this process is to put yourself in the shoes of your customers. One way to do this is to form a buyer persona based on their problems. Who are the people who face the problem you solve? How old are they? What interests them? You can design your customer's world based on your idea once you have stood in the shoes of your future customers. Ideally, this is the problem you are seeking to solve. To this end, Strategizer AG conceptualised the 'Business Model Canvas' and the 'Business Value Proposition Canvas'.

Here are several questions to help you create your business canvas:

- What are the negative trends in your market?
- What are the positive trends in your market?
- What headaches do people in your market have?

- What needs do people in your market have?
- What opportunities do people in your market have?
- What fears do people in your market have?
- What hopes do people in your market have?

Using Mind Maps™ and looking at the big picture

Once you've finished generating ideas, you need to map them out in a clear way to understand them. Mind Maps™ are a unique creative tool that should give you the confidence to explore and express your ideas in full. Created by author and consultant Tony Buzan, they allow you to visualise the connection between your ideas, discover which ones are the most important and find out which ones go together. They can also help you map out a project, process, or framework. It's comforting to know that, when we express our thoughts, we can create new possibilities by 'connecting the dots' between them. Mind Maps™ are useful to gain structure and confidence to develop ideas based on our identity.

What makes Mind Maps™ valuable is that they simplify your thoughts. Mind Maps™ don't tell you, 'this is too hard,' 'too risky' or 'too complex.' In fact, Mind Maps™ do the opposite. They show you how simple your ideas really are, and they conceptualize them in a way that's easy for anyone to understand. Mind Maps™ use the creative part of our brains and allow us to create structure. I highly encourage the use of Mind Maps™ to make sense of your ideas. At the end of the day, you are the answer, and exposing the logical structure of your ideas will help you extract the most value out of them.

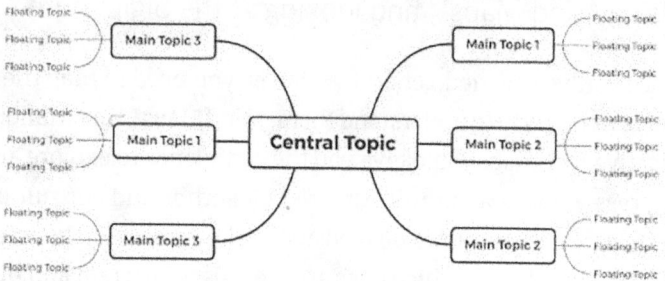

This is an example of a Mind Map created with the software XMind.

When working with ideas, it's important to keep an eye on the big picture. Without the big picture—whether it's in the form of Mind Maps™ or another creative tool—you risk getting lost at sea without ever finding your way back. At least fifty percent of all businesses fail within the first three to five years. Why is that the case? It's because entrepreneurs tend to get caught up in the details and forget the big picture. They also tend to overcomplicate their idea or business model. Complexity and perfectionism kill more business ideas than anything else combined.

Case study: Canva

The graphic design app Canva is an incredible success story. It demonstrates one woman and her team's foresight and hard work in solving a problem. Together, they created a human-centred solution to the world of graphic design. The idea behind Canva began in 2006 and grew out of frustration. Back then, it was hard to teach the art of design with the confusing tools provided by large tech companies like Adobe. As a designer, Melanie Perkins was acutely aware of the importance of having easy-to-use tools, so she set out to make a better tool.

Before founding Canva, Mel Perkins found early success with a business called Fusion Books. This business still exists today, and it is the largest school yearbook publisher in Australia. Fusion Books also expanded to France and New Zealand. While this journey set Perkins up for success, she and her partner and co-founder Cliff Obrecht had a dream of solving the problem caused by complicated graphic design tools. With the explosion of social media only years behind them, they wanted to create something that would ease expression in the world of digital design. So Canva was born.

Perkins's identity was always centred around solving problems. Such discipline and tenacity foreshadowed her success. Her business Fusion Books was the beginning of this journey, but the big problem (often known to entrepreneurs as the 'big fat hairy audacious goal' or 'BFHAG' for short) was creating a tool that allows people to express their creativity. That problem was a cornerstone of Perkins' identity. She is, after all, a designer herself.

Canva's journey was a steep climb, starting far away from Silicon Valley's tech giants. Perkins was a student at Western Australia University in Perth, Australia. After gaining the attention of a Silicon Valley entrepreneur, she went all the way to San Francisco to present her idea. Along the way, she redesigned the pitch decks of Silicon Valley tech founders, who recognised her core skill and ability to assist others in expressing themselves. From there, Canva would only grow.

In eight short years, Canva's intellectual property has been enshrined in trademarks, patents and designs. They hold at least sixty worldwide trademarks and twenty-five patents on Canva's unique functionality (including their graphical user interface). They have also created licensing arrangements with footage libraries, designers, and illustrators from all over the world. Identity has been core to Canva's success because Melanie, since she was a young child, was helping others express themselves through creativity. As of October 2021., Perkins and her team are known for having founded a unicorn now valued at AU$55 billion, making them the world's most valuable startup after Tik Tok, Stripe, and Space X.[iv]

Action Steps

This is your time to identify the idea you want to pursue. Identifying your idea is similar to building your boat. After all, the boat you build will have a major impact on your journey.

- Complete the following steps to figure out your idea before moving to the next step on the Ideaology compass.
- Find out your Enneagram type by taking the Enneagram Personality test: https://tests.enneagraminstitute.com/.

- What would you say your purpose is? This is rarely a job title. Think about the things you like to do and the skills that come naturally to you.
- What is the problem that you wish to seek in the world?
- Answer the questions from the Business Canvas.
- Design a mind map based on your ideas with a mind mapping software such as XMind.
- How does the problem defined in the Mind Maps and the Business Model Canvas relate?
- Does this idea fulfil your purpose?

References

[i] 'Blue Ocean Strategy.' https://www.blueoceanstrategy.com/what-is-blue-ocean-strategy/, (accessed August 1, 2021)

[ii] Mohit, Aron, 'Why Google Yahoo in the way for the Internet.' *TechCrunch*. https://techcrunch.com/2016/05/22/why-google-beat-yahoo-in-the-war-for-the-internet/, (accessed August 1, 2021).

[iii] The Enneagram Institute, 'The Nine Enneagram Type Descriptions.' https://www.enneagraminstitute.com/type-descriptions, (accessed August 1, 2021).

[iv] Waters, Cara. 'Canva founders to put their billions to good use.' https://www.smh.com.au/business/entrepreneurship/bigger-than-telstra-canva-s-valuation-doubles-in-five-months-to-55-billion-20210915-p58rq1.html, (Accessed October 1, 2021).

POINT 2: DEVELOP YOUR IDEA

'There is one thing stronger than all the armies in the world, and that is an idea whose time has come.' –Victor Hugo

Once you've identified the idea you want to pursue, you need to make the expression of it unique and tangible. This is not about making the idea a physical product—at least, not yet. It's about developing your idea in a way that's compelling to your audience. We refer to this process as developing heroic currency. You can use this process to express your idea in a unique way that is compelling enough to attract funding, prospects and supporters. This begins with the ancient craft of storytelling. While your idea is the boat that takes you to success, the story underlying it is the steam engine that propels it.

There's nothing more real to us humans than stories. There's nothing more compelling than being the hero in one, too. We make sense of the world through storytelling, and we make decisions based on the emotions we feel. All living cultures in the world have used storytelling to express their ideas. Think about it: You've been told stories since you were born.

The Rainbow Serpent is a unifying story of creation embraced by almost all Aboriginal Australian cultures. Tribes tell this story at the beginning and end of the day to describe the majestic colours that encircle the sky, also a symbol of death and rebirth. They use it to explain and reason their existence and to connect to their 'Dreamtime', which connects them to their ancestors and sense of purpose in the world. It guides them and their personal narrative in their resourceful search for purpose and meaning across vast tracts of land and to survive in the harsh outback of Australia.

In a similar way, you need to understand your journey as an entrepreneur by reflecting on your past to be in control of your present and design your future. Developing your idea includes the skill of defining the narrative that drives your business. This is necessary to survive and thrive in sometimes adverse conditions. Understanding and defining your own heroic journey will help you stay on course and succeed in your business endeavours. In this chapter, you will learn how to develop your idea and story in four steps:

1. Map out your customer's journey
2. Understand the elements of heroic currency
3. Develop the narrative of your business
4. Turn your journey into heroic currency

Map out your customer's journey

To begin the process of connecting your idea to what customers want, you need to examine the underlying story behind it and where it will take your audience. Storytelling has existed since the beginning of time. From Jesus Christ to the Kabala, our existence has been continually informed by the stories behind ideas. As every generation, so the adage says, 'we stand on the shoulders of the giants before us'. It is stories that contain the wisdom and learning that are passed through people, and their legacy can still be relevant to us in a present-day context.

To start with the story is to examine the key and recurring problems that have impacted our lives. It informs how we present these ideas to future audiences and generations; it helps us create purposeful intellectual property and allows us to commercialise ideas for our growth and that of others. The first tool you need to map out your prospect's story is the idea-journey map. It's a tool that can take many forms but that typically appears as some type of infographic. (You'll see an example later in this chapter.) Whatever its form, the goal is the same: to visualise the adaptation of your ideas to create a great customer experience.

The process of building an idea-journey map will help you to understand what questions users have and how the idea may solve the problem in the world. If you are part of an organisation, the idea-journey map can give managers an overview of the customer's experience. You can also use this to see how future customers move through your sales channels.

It's easy to craft ideas into meaningful experiences by translating thoughts into a three-act play. William Shakespeare mastered this art. In fact, his intellectual property was so popular that only a few theatres were permitted to perform his valuable copyright work.[i] The three-act play influenced theatre in his time and cinematic experiences in the hundreds of years to follow. In Ancient Greece, Aristotle was also keen on the three-act structure. We can use the three-act play to structure our ideas around purpose. By beginning with a three-act play, we are, quite simply, calling on the genetic code of storytelling that remains strong in the heart and mind of all human civilisation.

Starting with a story is to identify purpose in our ideas unfold as they unfold in three parts:

Beginning: This is where your idea is set up. We define this as a problem in the world, one that people can relate to. Such problems include environmental destruction, lack of clean water, poor internet access or the education system's shortcomings. Begin with the problem and you will embark on the journey.

Middle: This is where the journey of solving the problem takes place. Has clean water been solved in other ways? Does hydrogen energy or electric cars provide a better solution? Will the Internet of Things (IoT) improve our connectivity across multiple electronic devices? Or will augmented reality change the classroom forever? The journey is often the project or minimum viable product or concept. It is a journey to explore solving this idea and to create something new.

End: The end is the planned conclusion. Does the resolution of the problem save the world from human degradation? Does it lead to more human experiences around technology? Does it improve the quality of life of six billion people and counting?

This is the end of the story, and in human design thinking, we should always have the end in mind throughout the process.

Once you've defined the three-act structure for your idea, you need to use the elements of great storytelling to strengthen it and develop the heroic currency behind the idea. Heroic currency comes to life when you leverage storytelling in such a way that your customer become the hero of a compelling adventure.

Understand the elements of heroic currency

The three-act structure is the backbone of your story. Without it, your story cannot hold together. However, once you have a three-act structure, you need to add the elements that make your brand unforgettable to your audience. These elements are the details that make the difference between mediocrity and commercial success.

What's the point? Know what you intend to convey both narratively and emotionally. You should be able to describe the essence of your characters' transformation in one sentence and the emotional tone in a couple of words. For example, if your product or service is designed to help entrepreneurs deal with getting overwhelmed, your point might be to show the ease with which an entrepreneur can get rid of stress and anxiety.

Be authentic: Stories are more powerful when they include references to you and your identity. Honest expression is stronger and more resonant than clichés. Remember that people identify more with stories of failure than stories of success.

It's simply because we encounter more failures than successes throughout our life. Talking about your own failures is a great way to build rapport with your audience.

Have strong characters: Characters are a great vehicle to express deep human needs and generate empathy and interest from your audience. Focus on the characters of your story. Who are they? Where do they come from? What are their strengths and weaknesses? Think about the types of characters your audience would relate to. In any story, we must be able to identify with the characters and cheer for them.

Emotional details: Behind all behaviour lies emotion. What details can you share about your characters and their situation that will suggest the emotions that lie beneath? The emotions your characters feel will be felt by your audience. The more emotions you can make your audience feel, the better off you are because people make decisions based on emotions. Simply stated, the character goes on a psychological journey and moves from one emotional state to another during the three acts.

With the three-act structure and the elements of great story-telling, you are on track to create a powerful narrative for your idea. With such a narrative, you will be able to speak not only to your audience's mind but also to their heart. At the very core of business is emotions, the states your prospects want to escape from as well as the states they want to get to. To create successful intellectual property, you must make clear what these states are and how your audience can move from one to the other.

The adventure of your venture

To be successful as an entrepreneur, you too need to undertake a *heroic journey*—a journey filled with obstacles. This is a compelling part of your own personal narrative. The heart of any venture you take is called the 'road of trials', where, namely, you find all the obstacles you must overcome. Overcoming obstacles along the road of trials is one of the arduous tasks of the entrepreneur. Sometimes, we only discover we are heroes when we get disillusioned enough with the dysfunction of our present circumstances to change them. But when we feel sad, lost and hopeless enough, something deep within us can emerge, something stronger and wiser than we have ever known. We all have this heroic capacity within us. That is heroic currency.

Most people agree that creating a 50-million-dollar business is near impossible. But there is a man who not only achieved this, but who also did it from an internationally famous trademark. Founder and chairman of Bridge Climb Australia Paul Cave commercialised one of Australia's most famous landmarks: the Sydney Harbour Bridge. It took Cave almost ten years of planning to commercialise his idea, the Sydney Bridge Climb, alongside the trademark 'have the climb of your life.' Cave made no fewer than 52 presentations in the late 1990s. Through these presentations, he raised the $12 million he needed to fund the business that would enable millions of people to climb the Sydney Harbour Bridge.

What is most interesting about Paul's success is not the licensing of one of Australia's largest and significant trademarks and building icons. Rather, it is that his business proposition and

sales channel are driven by others, who make heroes of themselves. Capitalising on an internationally famous landmark he
didn't own while monopolising its iconography, Cave was able
to create an experience that is the envy of the world. All 1438
steps enable others to truly marvel at the incredible visions
of standing on the top of the Harbour Bridge. Much of the
leverage and the trademark rests in the enduring *heroic journey*
of building something truly unique. This naturally requires
persistence and determination.

Like the view from the bridge, Cave's personal and business
story is impressive. Paul made his mark as both a marketing
and general manager, founding and building the Amber Group
over twenty-two years, and acting as a non-executive director
of Domino's Pizza. He is the son of a Sydney-born tradesman
and was always told to do well at school, study hard and
go to university. He did so willingly while he acknowledged
that beyond the corporate world, there was another world
waiting for him as an entrepreneur. The vision for Bridge Climb
began after conducting a YPO (Young Presidents Organisation)
World Congress in 1989, which included a climb of the famous
landmark. It was then, on that call to adventure, that Paul's
great vision was founded, taking almost a decade to 'build the
bridge.'

Unfortunately, after a twenty-year reign, Cave lost the right to
operate Bridge Climb when the New South Wales government
awarded the licence to another business.[ii] But while it lasted,
Cave's empire was truly remarkable. Cave didn't have to pay
for any advertising, and the business sent personally delivered
word-of-mouth recommendations through one million cus-

tomers across the world, all of whom were enamoured by the adventure of conquering the bridge and to 'make heroes of themselves.' In the end, Cave was forced to move on to other ventures, but such is the nature of the world. We don't undertake the heroic journey just once. We do so for every idea we pursue.

This is what the building process is like. It takes time to perfect success, and sometimes, it requires having others around you to ensure your success. The good news is that you can use failure to help you succeed. On the road to success, you will inevitably encounter hurdles, big and small, real or imagined.

Turn your narrative into heroic currency

Joseph Campbell defined a classic sequence of actions found in many stories. He described it first in his book *A Hero with a Thousand Faces* (1949) and then in *The Power of Myth* (1988). Towards the end of his life, when he was interviewed by PBS journalist Bill Moyers, he demonstrated this powerful idea to a larger audience. In his work, Joseph Campbell reveals the universal truth that exists in stories. He calls it the 'Monomyth,' suggesting there is only one story in the world.

George Lucas, the ideaologist of the *Star Wars* series, used the structure of the hero's journey structure in creating the modern mythology in the *Star Wars* films. Luke Skywalker follows the epic hero's journey classically. So does Neo in *The Matrix* as he pursues his quest for liberation from his own mind. So, too, does Simba in *The Lion King* as he undertakes the journey of learning his true power. Likewise, Sam Worthington's character in *Avatar* goes from a disabled war veteran to an environmental warrior, a move that emulates the character's psyche and power.

This story, the heroic journey, has been repeated timelessly across cultures and ages. Campbell proved his monomyth theory by referencing stories from around the world and his thought leadership influenced popular culture. The hero's journey applies both to the entrepreneur's journey and the prospect's journey. Their journey unfolds as follows (from the entrepreneur's perspective):

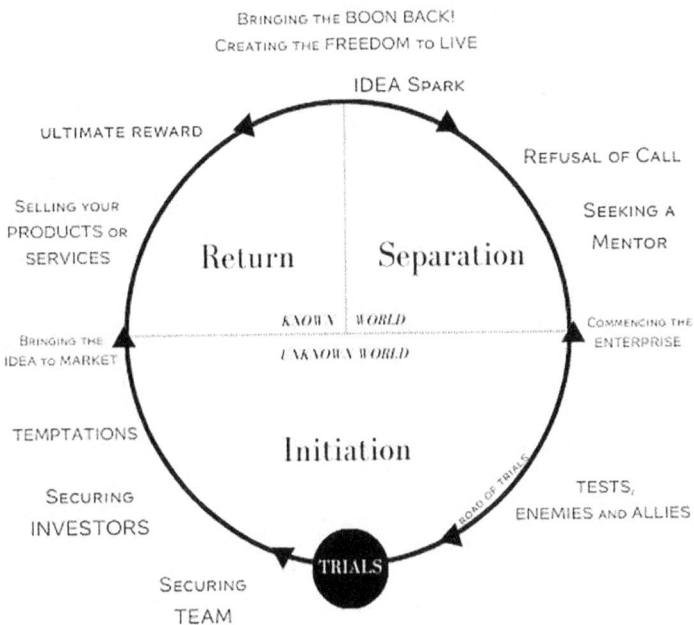

Idea spark: This is the stage of the journey where we first conceive the notion of our idea. This process of ideation is where we begin to conceptualise ideas that solve problems. This process may begin with a sketch on a napkin, a business plan, a Mind Map™ or another creative tool. However, there are many sure-fire ways to make sure this is an idea worth spreading; we explored these ways in the last chapter.

Call to action: The call to adventure happens when we decide to follow our purpose and our passion to create the solution to the problem. If we decide to be true to our identity and pursue our idea relentlessly, we are on the right path to solving a problem that can bring commercial success.

Seeking a mentor: As we embark on this journey, it's important to seek mentors who will encourage us along the way. Mentors can be people you meet synchronistically or through the adventure along the road of trials. When you meet them, take their advice kindly. There will be pitfalls, challenges and setbacks. Heed their advice and follow their suggestions. Perhaps it's the reason that you have started reading this book.

Commencing the enterprise: Making our first move is the most courageous step in this journey, and it begins with registering a domain name, a trademark and a business name. It also begins with research and discussions with industry leaders on how to implement the idea. It's the conviction to follow the idea and what it represents that matters the most. The path you chose is a challenging one, so brace yourself for the adventure. You will need heroic currency, resilience and determination to see this project through.

Tests, enemies and allies: This part of the journey brings a sense of discovery and invention that can create an enterprise. This is what some people call the innovation process. This may result in trials, sprints, and prototype development; it's about testing the idea for weaknesses and can involve its elaboration in new, unique ways. Intellectual property law will respect the inventiveness of these ideas when a new idea is made; it's necessary to ensure the idea is properly developed before it is enshrined and protected with registrations.

Discovery: Discovery can be accidental, but it is never incidental. A new idea or discovery means no one else has invented it, and sometimes, the real discovery isn't your original idea; it's what your idea led you to. If you make such a discovery, it's important to keep the method of the idea and to also register the idea. A patent or design registration helps protect this idea if it is deemed to be useful and inventive. (This means that skilled people in your industry would not find your invention an obvious thing to do.)

Ordeal, death and rebirth: Even when the inventive process takes a wrong turn, it's important to recognise that an ordeal has both a death and a rebirth. It is sometimes when the idea seems to be a struggle (i.e., in seeking investment or leveraging the rights to create new value) that we redefine it and improve it the most. For some, the struggle pertains to the protection of their intellectual property, while for others the struggle has to do with branding or development.

Reward, leverage and licensing: This is the process where we reap the rewards. Once an idea is enshrined into intellectual property, it can be leveraged, licensed, bought and sold. Be aware of instruments, such as terms and conditions of sales, that are a part of the process. It is the licensing of your goods and services that make transacting your intellectual property valuable and tangible. This is when it makes sense to engage with a qualified commercial and intellectual property professional to protect, value and leverage your idea for greater growth.

Seizing the sword for product growth: Once you have a marketable product, this is where seizing the sword and product growth happens. It's where genuine and tangible growth occurs, and you are rewarded for your efforts. This can happen when you have tested the marketplace and you know you have an identifiable market. It's about selling and reselling the goods and services and bringing them out to market. It's where your heroic currency will truly be tested and rewarded. This is also where your ideas gain market traction.

Bringing the boon back: This is the ultimate goal. It's when our identity is forged through successful business ownership. It's important to celebrate success. And as most serial entrepreneurs know, the journey will repeat itself into a new iteration of ideas and value creation.

Once you are aware of the stories contained in your idea and your entrepreneurial journey, you are set to develop the intellectual property you need to successfully commercialise your ideas. Intellectual property should be considered a key strategic process. Almost every organisation has an intellectual property portfolio of some value and therefore the need for an intellectual property strategy. A brand, for example, is an important form of intellectual property, as is any information managed and produced by an organisation. In the next chapters, we will elaborate how you can implement an intellectual property strategy by leveraging different tools and business approaches.

Case study: Apple

Apple is the best example of powerfully leveraged ideas and intellectual property. One of the most valuable businesses in the world, the trials and tribulations of Steve Jobs, defined the company to a large extent. Jobs had the heroic currency to identify opportunities and bring them to life. The consistency of his heroic currency enabled him to turn valleys into peaks and almost always brought back to economic success. His biography, written by Walter Isaacson, testifies how he shaped, if not created, no less than seven major industries:

1. *Computing*
2. *Animated movies*
3. *Music*
4. *Phones*
5. *Tablet computing*
6. *Digital publishing*
7. *Retailing*

Jobs' biography reveals how every time he failed (including when he was removed from the board of the company he founded), he set sights on new successes. Some may not recognise that he founded Pixar Studios and used his heroic currency to reinvent the studio that has rivalled Disney. The intellectual property that he created as a result (across trademarks, patents, designs, source code, and copyright) is worth billions of dollars today. His journey, one of tenacity, brilliance and design should be recognised for its boldness and courage. This is the journey of one individual, a man as iconic as the Apple Trademark itself.

Such is the power of heroic currency.

Action Steps

- Ask yourself how you can make your customer or user a hero of the idea.
- Examine the concept of heroic currency and apply it to yourself and your business.
- Ask yourself where you currently are in the heroic journey of your enterprise.
- Ponder how you will leverage your ideas for further growth.
- Name three products and services that have created true value in your life.
- Ask how you will create true value for the user and the future.

References

[i] Britannica, 'Globe Theatre.' https://www.britannica.com/topic/Globe-Theatre, (accessed August 1, 2021).

[ii] Thomsen, Simon. 'END OF AN ERA: Sydney BridgeClimb founder Paul Cave just lost the right to his famous business.'

https://www.businessinsider.com.au/sydney-harbour-bridgeclimb-paul-cave-tender-lost-2018-6, (accessed August 1, 2021).

POINT 3: EXPRESS YOUR IDEA

'No matter what people tell you, words and ideas can change the world.' —Robin Williams

What do you think Apple, Amazon, Google and Microsoft all have in common? You are right to think they are some of the marketplace's biggest tech titans ruling in the fourth industrial revolution. But they are also the world's most valuable trademarks and brands. As of 2021, Apple and Amazon are both valued in the trillions of dollars.[i] Amazon and Apple's brand value greatly impact the marketplace, and they demonstrate the important role that brands play in a company's valuation. In a market driven by new technology and new ideas, intellectual property is everything.

In an Ideas Economy, it's not enough to simply identify and develop ideas. To find true commercial success and build wealth, we need to *express* these ideas. This is where intellectual property comes in.

Think of your business as a sailing ship. Underneath the deck, placed within the secure hold, you have many ideas worthy of your protection as valuable cargo. To understand this analogy, we need to explore every aspect of intellectual property, beginning by exploring copyright. In this chapter, we will also explore how to protect your most vital assets, your ideas, through the following registrable instruments:

1. Copyright
2. Trademarks
3. Designs
4. Patents
5. Contracts

Your intellectual property should always be secured in one place. If you are building a business, it makes sense to register your IP in the name of your propriety limited company. Doing so builds your business and secures your IP. It means that your business grows in value. It also protects you, as it's safely secured in a separate legal entity.

Other benefits of registering your intellectual property with your business include limited liability and more friendly taxation. There are a lot of benefits to registering your IP, but there are a lot of potential conflicts around ownership. Suffice to say, if you are the captain of your ideas, you will keep all your valuable cargo in your hold.

Copyright

Copyright is the foundation of our intellectual property laws. It emerged at the same time as the printing press in the late 16th century. The printing press enabled writers to share their works and protect their pecuniary interests. Back then, many writers' guilds accepted manuscripts with a post and date mark so writers could prove their work's provenance (now known as a priority date).

Defensible under the *Copyright Act 1968,* Copyright has since extended to film, sound recordings, animation and 3D objects to name a few. The pecuniary rights of copyright holders now extend beyond their death in common law countries—70 years after the author's death. Copyright protection is one of the most automatic forms of IP as it is protected as soon as it is created.

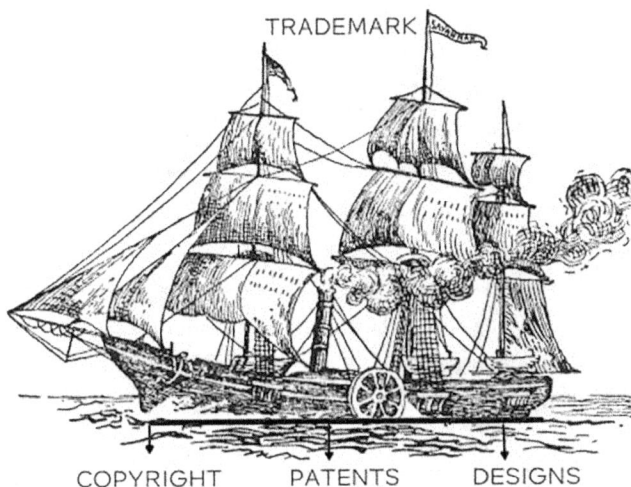

TRADEMARK

COPYRIGHT   PATENTS   DESIGNS

In the Ideas Economy, copyright extends so much further than the written word. It extends to your digital assets such as your website copy and images, social media platforms, marketing collateral, business plans and content. Copyright is also data, and data is a hallmark of a big business. Therefore, it serves you to understand all the copyright in your business, including your physical assets (books, business plans and business cards, for example). Like any good ship captain, you should always know what assets you have under your hold. And in the Ideas Economy, this includes all your ideas that are your treasures.

Traditional Copyright Materials	Digital Copyright Materials
• Business plans	• Source code
• Schematics	• Software
• Written concepts	• Computer programs
• Books	• Website
• Marketing materials (copy, photographs, videos, etc.)	• Social platforms
• Databases	• Customized Software
• Customer lists	• Data

Your first step in creating intellectual property is to safely secure all the copyright in your business. This may be as simple as making a list, what we call an 'IP asset register'. Your list can also be more thorough, including the terms and conditions on your website, your privacy policy, your end-user licence agreement and your brand agreements. At the end of the day, all your intellectual property assets need to be secured and protected in the hold of your boat for you to sail into the seas of success.

Copyright and data

As mentioned earlier, in an Ideas Economy, data is a hallmark of a big business. Data is copyrighted material as it is owned by various users. Digital businesses produce data, and it is important to understand the various roles that data can play in business. Data can be broadly considered as:

- **Public Data:** Information publicly available but used in a business context, such as the weather or industrial information.
- **Customer Data:** Information of users and personnel that use your products or services, e.g., email databases.
- **Private Data:** Commercially sensitive information not available to the public that can be secured by encryption and backed up.
- **Treated Data:** Information used and licensed as part of software-as-a-service, considered sensitive commercial data. This is big business, in terms of software solutions

As you may appreciate as an Ideaologist, such copyright information is important and valuable in the Ideas Economy. The role of licensing has never been more important, as well as the value of the privacy of this information and its copyright. (Which may be the subject of another book!)

'Intellectual property is the oil of the 21st century,' said Mark Getty. 'Look at the richest men a hundred years ago: They all made their money extracting natural resources or moving them around. All today's richest men have made money out of intellectual property.'

Case Study: Mark Getty and Getty Images

Getty Images is one business that has successfully leveraged copyright in business. One of its co-founders, Mark Getty, happens to be the grandson of some of the richest oil tycoons on the planet. Mark Getty, a passionate photographer and artist, leveraged his identity into a new abundant resource: intellectual property.

Getty Images, Inc. (stylised as gettyimages) is a supplier of stock images, editorial photography, video and music for business and consumers. It owns an archive of over 200 million assets. It targets three markets—creative professionals (advertising and graphic design), the media (print and online publishing), and corporate (in-house design, marketing and communication departments). Getty has offices around the world and capitalises on the internet for distribution.

As Getty has acquired other older photo agencies and archives, it has digitised their collections, which enabled online distribution. Getty Images operates a large commercial website that clients use to search and browse for images, purchase usage rights and download images. Getty's power has been the licensing of people's copyrighted images for a fee. Leveraging copyright through online digital libraries during the rise of social media created a multimillion-dollar business in a matter of years. The powerhouse was then sold for 3.3 billion dollars in 2012, which demonstrates the power of copyright and how licensing intellectual property assets can create a success powerhouse.

Trademarks

If copyright is stored safely in the hold of your ship, your trademark is the flag that flies high above your ship. A trademark should be hoisted high on the mast of your business and is immediately recognisable to your customers and competitors. Defensible by law under the *Trademarks Act 1995*, a trademark is a badge of origin, the beacon that calls for customers to engage with your business. The flag and name of your business identify your product or service in the marketplace, both online and offline. It continually surprises me that people can be the captain of their idea, sometimes for several years, and still not be aware that they have not registered their most visible and important asset—trademark. They are effectively sailing an unregistered vessel and leaving their name and cargo exposed to the rest of the world.

You wouldn't build a boat without ensuring it is seaworthy, so why would you begin sailing without protecting your most visible asset: your brand? Many business owners are under the misguided impression that registering their domain and business names protects their brand. It does not. In the ever-changing branding environment, your trademark is your most vital asset. Your brand, embodied and protected with a trademark, is the distinctive value through which your brand gets noticed. It serves you to protect this with a registered trademark as many businesses have done before you. This can protect your business, its name and legal recognition in the marketplace for at least 10 years.

Consider the value of brands such as Facebook, Uber and Airbnb. These businesses did not exist 25 years ago, and they have more than one competitor. What makes them so valuable? Their intellectual property portfolio of copyright (including massive amounts of data), trademarks, patents and designs. The likes of Facebook, Uber and Airbnb have successfully expressed their solution to a problem, protected their assets and offered value to the marketplace. As times change, Richard Branson once remarked, customers and employees connect with brands, not corporations. As a result of this changing landscape, it is imperative to protect the value of your brand and your intellectual property. If you have been in business for more than one year, then you have intellectual property worthy of protection. If you seek to build your business into an empire worth millions of dollars, it is imperative that you have an IP strategy in place to protect, value and leverage your assets. The propensity of these ideas to create leverage and change is crucial in an Ideas Economy. Your brand, your most visible intellectual property, must be protected.

Having a registered trademark is just the beginning when it comes to protecting the valuable intellectual property a business owns. A brand can also be protected through other registrations such as designs, patents and even plant breeders' rights. Like copyright, these provisions should all be stowed safely under the deck of your business as it contributes to the valuable cargo that you can trade around the world. It also allows you to draw a map (otherwise known as an IP strategy) to protect and build trade routes for your valuable cargo.

What can I trademark?

A trademark identifies your unique product or service in the marketplace. A good trademark distinguishes your business from other traders in the marketplace. Your trademark is not limited to the name, the logo or even the tagline of your product or service. It can also include:

- a letter
- a number
- a word
- a phrase
- a sound
- a smell
- a shape
- a picture
- a movement
- an aspect of packaging or a combination of these.
- A 3D object

Sometimes referred to as a brand, your trademark helps your customers discern the quality of your product or service over that of your competition. All these aspects of marketing and branding collateral can be protected and are enforceable in Australia under the *Trademarks Act 1995*. A trademark is the only legal instrument that can protect your business name, including your domain name. Trademarks can identify an organisation as a source of products and services, which is a critical part of its branding and marketing purposes. In an age of digital disruption, which is part of the Ideas Economy, the recognition of a brand becomes even more important in an evolving marketplace. Disney, Marvel and Qantas are great examples of trademarks that have continued to grow in value over the last 100 years.

Trademark laws differ between common law countries, but registering in your home country (e.g., Australia) means you gain access to important international reciprocal rights through a treaty known as the Madrid Protocol, which will protect your brand in 115 member countries around the world, including the U.S., the U.K., and Europe. Trademarks are applied for and registered in 'classes' of similar goods and services, and it is very important to ensure that, upon lodgement of your trademark, the correct goods and services are applied for. If in doubt, seek advice from a qualified intellectual property professional. Only a trademark grants full protection of ownership of the legal business name and should be one of the first things that are considered once branding your idea for greater commercial growth.

Is my business protected if I register the domain name?

Business, company or domain names are very different from trademarks. Domains are effectively licensed names (i.e., a domain) from a domain registry. Your annual renewal fee is just that: a license fee. Only a registered trademark gives you the exclusive legal right to use your name. If someone infringes your trademark by copying it, or using it without your permission (online, offline or even in new virtual worlds like Augmented or Virtual Reality), you have the legal right to stop them. Business, company or domain names do not provide this sort of protection.

There are no time limits on the registration of a trademark, but delays leave the door open for a third party to register a 'blocking mark', preventing you from using your own brand. To build your brand identity, try to secure the same name for your trademark and your business or company name. Brand owners should first do a free search on the Trademark register to make sure their brand name is available.

Case study: Virgin v. Virgin Sumo

Early in my career as a practicing lawyer, I took on a pro bono case for a Sydney music band. The band was named Virgin Sumo, and the members wore university polo shirts. They were students playing in Glebe and other suburbs as part of Sydney's band scene. Unbeknownst to them, they were about to walk into trouble with one of the most protected brands on the planet, Virgin.

One of the testimonies to Richard Branson's success, who began building his empire with Virgin Records (subsequently Virgin Music), has been the cumulative effect of building and leveraging one of the most effective brands in the world, Virgin, into almost every category of brand protection imaginable. Virgin is registered in almost every category of goods and services with IP Australia. At the last count, Virgin has at least 258 registrations in Australia and there are over 4000 registrations of names and symbols of this name worldwide. In fact, Virgin's brand strategy (apart from Richard Branson's excellent personal brand and unconventional PR style, which makes business fun) is to leverage the power of the brand into new business industries. Virgin sells everything from credit cards to cola to flights. Now an international brand, Virgin is highly protective of its trademark as are others such as Disney, Harley Davidson, Microsoft and Apple.

Virgin Sumo experienced Virgin's protective brand strategy firsthand. The band received several 'cease and desist' notices, which required the members to stop using this name as it was a protected name of Virgin Australia. Although the members eventually folded, they were concerned they would lose the value of their brand, which they had built over several years. Adopting a win-win strategy to intellectual property negotiation, I was able to negotiate a settlement with Richard Branson's company for the band to drop the name 'Virgin' in return for a $5,000 settlement, which was enough for them to record their first studio album.

Designs

While a trademark protects a brand by making it recognisable in the marketplace, a design protects the visual appearance of a product. The registration of an industrial design right can be made together with trademark protection. While a trademark typically protects a logo and brand, design rights protect the look, feel and shape of a product. It is important to distinguish design rights from patents at the outset. Designs protect the look and feel of a product's visual appearance whilst a patent protects the operations and functionality of a product.

Registering and certifying a design can be a lengthy, complex and costly process, especially if you're planning on commercialising your design. The commercial design development process can typically involve as many as five professional advisers or consultants. They could include specialists such as industrial designers, lawyers, marketing consultants and accountants. These advisers make separate contributions to the design process. Advice from all professionals may be required to successfully complete a design application, registration and commercialisation.

A design right protects the overall visual appearance of new and distinctive products. The overall visual appearance can be a combination of these visual features:

- shape
- colour
- configuration
- pattern
- ornamentation

It is an important distinction that a design right protects the visual appearance of a whole product that has a physical and tangible form, whether manufactured or handmade. Design protection allows the design to be protected in order to be scaled for commercial production. This requires working with an IP specialist who will assist you in articulating the novelty and distinctiveness of your Design as defined in the *Designs Act 2003*. Once protected, the design will be registered in Australia for 5 years. Like trademarks, you can extend the protection of this right overseas.

Patents

A patent is a legally enforceable and exclusive right to commercially exploit an invention for a specific period. Patents are the most complex and expensive forms of intellectual protection. Patent law provides an incentive for innovation on a global scale because they ensure the exclusivity of use. Today, companies such as Apple still rely on patents to protect their market share. The most valuable patents are those that cover best-selling products (e.g., the iPhone), and they are difficult to replicate given their strong protection in a number of different registrable forms, which includes their logo (Apple), their design (the iPhone) and their patents (unique functionalities of their products).

When it comes to innovation, patents are the key. Melanie Perkins, the founder of the graphic design app Canva, has 97 patents in her name. The same month as this book was published, the valuation of her business went from US$15 billion to US$55 billion. Canva's graphical interface is patented and allows the company to protect its unique way of helping users create graphical art with ease. Patents are one of the main reasons Canva was able to grow so much and so fast. See the next chapter to understand how registered intellectual property can amplify in value, once protected.

Not every invention is worth patenting, though. Patenting an invention can be prohibitively costly; it may be more cost-effective to rely on other forms of protection such as design rights or trade secrets. The 'scope' of a patent is an important indicator of value in that it determines the range of products that a patent owner may prevent from being sold. Unlike copyright, patent rights are not automatic and must be applied for at the Patent Office in each country where protection is sought.

A patent can be used to protect any idea involving 'human invention' leading to a new utility or new use. This means that anything which requires some human creativity and is practically useful can potentially be patentable. It is key to ensure that the invention contains a 'new' and 'inventive step'. This can include:

- A process or method (such as a new way to manufacture concrete)
- A machine (something with moving parts or circuitry)
- A manufactured article (such as a tool or another object that accomplishes a result with few or no moving parts, such as a pencil)
- A new composition (such as a new pharmaceutical)
- An asexually reproduced and new variety of plant.

There are some exclusions, such as scientific principles, dis-coveries (things that occur naturally but have only now been discovered), abstract ideas (such as a set of rules for playing a game) and intangible concepts (such as mathematical for-mula, purely abstract business methods, etc.) However, these excluded concepts may be patentable if they are used to produce some 'technical effect' or 'physical consequence.' In other words, if there is some perceptible alteration or change made to something, and it has commercial significance, then valid patent protection may still be possible. As each country in the world has its own patent laws, different countries generally have different approaches to what constitutes a patentable invention.

An application for patent protection can be made by one or more individuals, partners, companies, government entities or other legally recognised persons. However, for patent protection to be validly granted, the patent applicant must either be the inventor or must have derived rights to the invention, either directly or indirectly, from the inventor. If you are filing a patent application, beware of the risks of public disclosure. Public demonstration, sale or discussion of your invention before the filing of your patent may jeopardise your application.

Patent protection differs from one country to the other. In Australia, for example, there are two types of patents: standard patents and innovation patents. Standard patents offer the full protection allowable under law, while innovation patents offer a shorter period of protection for incremental product developments. The following are some key differences between the two types of patents:

Length of protection

Standard: 20 years from the filing date.

Provisional patent: 12 months from the filing date

Requirements

Standard: The invention must be both 'novel' (i.e., new) and involve an 'inventive step' (i.e., not obvious).

Provisional: The invention must be both 'novel' (i.e., involve an 'innovative step') but can be updated after 12 months.

Examination process

Standard: The application undergoes substantive examination process before grant.

Provisional: The application does not automatically undergo substantive examination before grant.

Enforceability

Standard: The patent is enforceable against others once granted.

Provisional: The patent is enforceable against others once a substantive examination is performed, and the patent is 'certified' by the Australian Patent Office.

A cautionary tale to protect your patents

One of the most innovative and ground-breaking inventions by our highest scientific and research organisation was never protected. Invented in the 1990s, WLAN was the scientific breakthrough that modernised computer networks. It was never protected by the CSIRO, and an American company was the first to commercialise the invention successfully. CSIRO sued and a settlement was made. However, their omission to protect their most important invention and commercialise it could have effectively created a Silicon Valley in Australia.

Early protection of intellectual property is always key. The earlier you protect your intellectual property assets, the fewer the risks to your company. This is a tale of caution: always seek legal advice with a significant invention and never published it until it is protected. This will ensure that your ship can be created into a fleet, or even an armada, that could lift the prosperity of an entire county.

Contracts

Contracts are very robust instruments that assist you in protecting your intellectual property and can take various forms. Contracts include your website's terms and conditions, privacy policy (required by law in Australia) as well as your contracts with customers and service providers. Intellectual property holds the same the relationship with your business as your physical property. For your business to achieve true success, it needs to be built on the firm foundations of contracts and intellectual property.

One of the key misconceptions I have observed as an IP specialist for the last 20 years is how little importance we attribute to the role that contracts play in the protection of registrable and non-registrable intellectual property. A contract is a legally binding document that outlines the terms and conditions between two parties. A contract can extend the legal obligation between two parties to the ownership and use of intellectual property. This can take shape in many different types of commercial (and non-commercial) agreements.

Some examples include:

- **Assignment agreement**: assigning intellectual property to another party.
- **Licensing agreement**: licensing intellectual property to another party (for a fee).
- **Joint venture agreement**: sharing intellectual property for the purpose of a business, project or enterprise.
- **Purchase agreement**: terms to purchase the intellectual property of another.
- **Franchise agreement**: agreement to franchise the intellectual property through a complex set of contracts in which a franchise will buy into the intellectual property of the owner and follow the rules of the franchise.

The role of contracts in intellectual property

The role of contracts should never be underestimated in protecting intellectual property. A contract is a powerful form of protection not only for registered IP (trademarks, designs and patents), but also for remaining as equally enforceable with respect to copyright. In fact, a contract remains the most robust instrument to protect your ideas. Intellectual property should always be properly secured by a contract. Beyond registrable rights, a contract is the strongest form of protection and leverage for intellectual property.

Chain of Title

Setting aside the ship metaphor for a moment and taking a look at another monument of industry, the chain of title is like the Burj Khalifa Tower in Dubai. It is the tallest building in the world. Watching the sunrise on the platform of this building is an awe-inspiring event. It towers into Dubai's skyline as a true giant with a grand perspective offered to the building innovations that surround it. As darkness turns to light, any human can only marvel at the impact of being so high. For this building to be built, it needed strong foundations and relationships between all its contractors. These were imperative to creating the platform of success to ensure that this building achieved its vision as the tallest building in the world. The Burj Khalifa Tower is a great analogy to think about contracts and the chain of title.

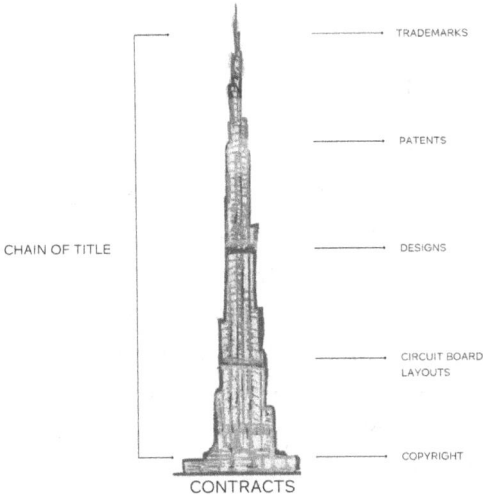

All business owners must own a chain of title for their intellectual property. A chain of title ensures that the property owner is the legal owner of all the assets of its business copyright, trademarks, designs and patents in their business. Your business is the robust tower which houses your intellectual property. And to ensure that you, the owner, have total control of the property, your business needs to be built on strong foundations. Otherwise, it may fall over in its attempts to reach the sky.

A Chain of Title of ownership is the same in property ownership as it is in intellectual property ownership. The business owner needs to ensure that the company's intellectual property and contracts are owned by the business owner to have property that it can sell. Even established businesses need to do a continual stocktake of its assets (and ideas) to ensure that they have valuable treasures to trade with the rest of the world.

IP Assessments

Businesses seeking to leverage their value with some of their core intellectual property assets should continually explore the protection of these elements. Many companies have intellectual property lying dormant. Without regular maintenance of their assets, these companies are unable to assess their true worth. It's also worth noting that these ideas can have new value in a new marketplace. A logo or brand could be licensed to a competitor to use for a fee. A patent could be sold or auctioned off to a start-up. Designs could be reengineered to create new products and create new value from existing ideas. This is the continual process of innovation, which is also a requirement in the Ideas Economy. An IP audit assists business owners and managers establish what IP assets they currently have and reassess their commercial pathways to continually create new value.

Action Steps

- Download the 2-page IP assessment available at garethbenson.com.
- Conduct an IP assessment of the intellectual property in your business including copyright, trademarks, designs, and patents.
- Ask yourself the following questions:
- Do you have any registered trademarks, designs or patents?
- What other intellectual property exists within your business? If the intellectual property is not registered, do you

own it?
- What is the chain of title and where do you store your intellectual property?
- Who has written and designed all your marketing and promotional material, including printed brochures and leaflets?
- Do you hold and maintain an IP asset register? If not have you considered an IP Audit or assessment of all your existing IP assets?
- Does your firm have policies and procedures in place specifically to manage and protect your IP?
- Do you have a staff education program that covers the management and protection of your IP?

References

[i] Forbes, 'The World's Most Valuable Brands.' https://www.forbes.com/powerful-brands/list/, (accessed August 1, 2021).

POINT 4: ASSESS YOUR IDEA

"Your wealth is in many ways dependent on what other people will pay for your assets." —Peter Bernstein

An often-neglected step in the entrepreneurial journey is the valuation of intellectual property. The days when we valued businesses purely on their physical assets are over. Although it may be counter-intuitive to you, valuing your business's intangible assets is one of the most critical steps in your entrepreneurial journey. It ensures that you have not only protected your assets, but that you are also leveraging them for financial gains. Valuation is what allows you to get the right price for shares of your business when looking for investors.

While valuation and exchange models have existed well before the invention of currency, the current Ideas Economy challenges traditional valuation methods. The internet has created highly efficient business models that make time and space are irrelevant and where the most valuable assets stay inside a computer. It is now possible to demonstrate the value of goods and services by effectively valuing intangible assets within your business.

This process may seem counter-intuitive and unnatural to you, but consider this: In life, if we do not consider our own inherent value, it is difficult for others to do so. Therefore, we must demonstrate our business's inherent value, especially to the audience with which we want to do business. While not easy, valuation is a crucial step for your business's growth. Valuation is what creates business juggernauts such as Apple, Amazon, Google and Microsoft.

Business valuation of intangible assets

In the last 25 years, the valuation of intangible assets increased to almost 80 percent of the total value of certain business types and industries. The value of the intangible assets owned by Fortune 500 companies alone is substantial. As Martha M. Rumore points out, 'Valuation of intellectual property rights is part of the good management of intellectual property within an organisation.'[i]

Indeed, the valuation of a business's intellectual property value should be at least an annual event. As Rumore also notes, 'Knowing the economic value and importance of the intellectual property rights you create and develop assists in the strategic decisions to be taken on the assets, but also facilitates the commercialisation and transactions concerning intellectual property rights.'[ii]

Rumore states four situations that require valuation:

1. Valuation of a company for the purposes of a merger, acquisition, joint venture or bankruptcy

2. Negotiations to sell or license intellectual property rights
3. Support in situations of conflict, such as court proceedings or alternative dispute resolution mechanisms (such as arbitration)
4. Fundraising through bank loans or venture capital.

Three approaches to valuing intellectual property

How exactly do you value your intellectual property assets? There are three different approaches you can apply to leverage intellectual property for financial gains. These methods aren't necessarily meant to be used in isolation; rather, they are meant to guide you in your business valuation by comparing different variables. After all, your business's value is determined by you and the other parties involved in the transaction. On the one hand, if you overvalue your business, you will likely face resistance from parties outside your business (e.g., investors or potential buyers). On the other hand, if you undervalue your business, the resistance will come from the parties inside your business (provided you have astute partners and advisors).

A. Cost Approach

The 'cost approach,' as the World Intellectual Property Organisation describes, 'establishes the value of an IP asset by calculating the cost of a similar (or exact) IP asset. The cost method is particularly useful when the IP asset can be easily reproduced and when the economic benefits of the asset cannot be accurately quantified.' That said, sunk costs and unique characteristics are not considered in the cost method.

The cost approach for IP valuation relies on data relating to the cost of replacing a product with a similar product. The cost approach is useful in situations where there is limited data available that would indicate the fair market value of the product. The cost approach considers the cost of labour and other direct expenditures such as consulting fees, research and development costs, prototype costs and other direct out-of-pocket expenses to redevelop the product.

For example, a trademark valuation using the cost approach might consider the legal costs of registering the trademark and promotional expenditures used to develop the brand name. The cost approach has a limited function because the economic benefits from IP do not always commensurate with the costs of developing the product. Its main use is in the preparation of notional valuations used to apportion the price of a business among its underlying assets.

B. Market Approach

The 'market approach' is another great approach to accelerate your growth. According to the World Intellectual Property Organisation, it is a method 'based on a comparison with the actual price paid for the transfer of rights to a similar IP asset under comparable circumstances."[iii] Unlike other methods, '[the market approach] has the advantage of being simple and based on market information, so it is often used to establish approximate values for use in determining royalty rates, tax, and inputs for the income method.'

The market approach values IP in terms of what a notional purchaser would pay for a substituted product and relies on empirical data obtained from arm's-length transactions in an open market. In other words, it determines value based on what a 'fair market' would pay. This is often the approach real estate and property developers use.

Usually, the valuation of the IP draws data from other companies that either make comparable products or are, at least, in the same industry as the IP's company. On the flip side, the market approach sometimes lacks available data on market transactions for similar products. IP often relates to technology that exists in a niche market, such as hospital diagnostic equipment. In such cases, it can be hard to find comparable products to use as a guideline. Moreover, the details contained in these transactions may not be publicly available.

C. Income Approach

The 'income approach' is the most used method for intellectual property valuation. It values IP assets on the amount of economic income the IP is expected to generate, adjusted to its present-day value. This method is easiest to use for intellectual property assets with positive cash flows or that are easy to assess and are reliable. The income approach provides a general, present-day value of the asset by considering the income expected to be generated from the ownership of the asset. Income approaches calculate future income-based valuation based on transactions around the IP.

The most popular methodology is the discounted cash flow method and methods derived from it. These methods usually have three variables:

1. Level of prospective income (cash flow)
2. Period of the income stream
3. The risk of achieving the prospective income level

The income approach may be used to measure long-term cash flows, particularly when they are not stable. Further Considerations Valuation approaches of IP, which consider performance outcomes, must take into account the strength and duration of the asset prior to estimation. Some forms of intellectual property (patents, trademarks, trade secrets and franchises) are more promising than others, and therefore capable of generating greater income.

One important concept to understand in valuation is 'goodwill'. Goodwill is an accounting term that refers to the intangible asset created by the difference between the price for which a company is acquired and its fair, normal market value as well as liabilities. 'Outside of accounting,' Harold Averkamp writes, 'goodwill might be referring to some value that has been built up within a company as a result of delivering amazing customer service, unique management, teamwork, etc. However, this goodwill is unrelated to a business combination and cannot be recorded or reported on the company's balance sheet.'[iv]

To better understand the three valuation approaches, think of the Titanic, which sank in the Atlantic Ocean in 1912 on its way to New York City from Southampton, England. Before it sank, you could value the Titanic based on how much it would cost to replace such an asset ($400 million in today's money).[v] But valuing the Titanic solely on its cost would leave money on the table. The Titanic transported 2,228 people, and ticket prices ranged from $1,700 to $50,000 in today's money.[vi] If the Titanic hadn't hit an iceberg, it would have kept generating revenues, thereby boosting the enterprise's value.

That said, with the market approach, the value of the Titanic could have fluctuated (again, assuming it hadn't sunk). If investors were willing to pay a price higher than normal for shares of the business, then the business's value increases. After all, the Titanic was the most luxurious ship of its time. Its value was almost priceless. However, after it sunk, it was effectively worthless. Today, all that's left of the Titanic are artefacts and James Cameron's billion-dollar movie (another great example of leveraging intellectual property).

Always make sure you keep your IP on the surface with valuation. In today's world, the market approach changes like the tides because markets are very volatile. It's important to stay afloat; all ships rise on a rising tide, and the valuation methods are instruments on the bridge to be used by the captain. In order to get financed or obtain venture capital, you need to answer this simple question—what is it worth? Your idea is worthy of not only your protection, but also your valuation. This will require research and analysis, and you can enrol the support of professional accountants and consultants who may assist you.

Case study: LinkedIn and historic Microsoft valuation

When Microsoft announced its $26 billion acquisition of LinkedIn in 2016, there had been predictable scepticism about how the company would recoup its investment.[vii] In fairness, the social network was known to be unprofitable. While LinkedIn had some synergies with its new parent, Microsoft, these synergies would unlikely be enough to justify the price tag in traditional terms.

Microsoft's acquisition of LinkedIn demonstrates the increasingly tangible value of intangible assets in a digital economy. Why? Because, for Microsoft and its existing enterprise solutions, LinkedIn's data acquisition engine and the digital assets it creates are uniquely valuable. LinkedIn is the only professional social network that has achieved meaningful scale, and the data it collects can be powerfully leveraged.

Back in 2016, LinkedIn had only just begun commercialising its intellectual property, with most of its current revenue coming in through recruiting services. To this day, LinkedIn holds a war chest of market-disruptive intellectual property that Microsoft values. This includes rich and relevant data on its business users, connections with professionals, resumes, work history, and traffic behaviour. Microsoft no doubt wanted to leverage and commercialise these assets. As such, this gamble could prove extremely valuable for Microsoft.

The US$26.2 billion valuation LinkedIn achieved equates to approximately 8.1 times LinkedIn's yearly revenues (US$3.2B) and delivers an impressive premium when compared to other listed companies (hovering around 5.1 times TTM revenue). The six months leading to

83

Microsoft's purchase of LinkedIn proved a window of opportunity for any of the tech titans to purchase a social network with almost half a billion users worldwide. Only shortly after the sale, we learned that Salesforce was engaged in a bidding war, which drove LinkedIn's price by almost US$5 billion.

Returns on the valuation

For Microsoft, the price paid for LinkedIn was likely to generate value in the following 3 to 5 years. It compared to Google's purchase of YouTube in 2008 and Facebook's purchase of in Instagram and WhatsApp in 2012 and 2014 respectively. Microsoft is known to leverage its new asset to generate strong cash flows and to complement and promote its enterprise solutions. The challenge for Microsoft would be to eclipse any of the valuation woes which LinkedIn suffered in the past and make up for it with advertising revenues. In 2021, though, Microsoft reported US$3 billion in ad revenues from LinkedIn, and this number is expected to keep growing.[viii]

From Windows to the Office Suite, to Azure and BASIC, Microsoft will no doubt continue to push assets such as their Surface tablet or Skype communications into professional-use cases. The company will also likely invest into projects which will power LinkedIn's powerful data for use by Microsoft's existing and emerging enterprise solutions. The purchase of LinkedIn was an exercise in the valuation of the goodwill of a business rich with intellectual property and could set a precedent for the valuation of intangible assets.

Although Peter Atwater wrote in *The Times* that the deal shows we overvalue goodwill[ix], I believe the LinkedIn purchase demonstrates our changing and, at times, misunderstood digital marketplace. Moreover, Microsoft's gamble is an expression of the exciting and pivotal locus we are now witnessing. The valuation of digital businesses and their capacity to generate cash flows ultimately dictate the economic drivers of our future.

Conclusion

While the valuation and accounting treatment of intellectual property have been traditionally an afterthought, the sheer value that tech businesses generate in short amounts of time demonstrates its increasing importance. The valuation of tech giant Atlassian, which clinched a record-breaking US$4.4 billion (AU$6.1 billion) valuation, is a testimony to the power of intellectual property growth that can be achieved in Australia.

The cost, market and income approaches each have their benefits and drawbacks when applied to valuing IP. The cost approach of valuing IP presents difficulties because the economic value to a company's IP is not necessarily represented by costs. Conversely, the market and income approaches are more suited for valuing IP in an ideas-and-innovation economy because they aim to reflect the economic worth, rather than the costs, of the IP. Valuing intellectual property should be a task that happens on a quarterly basis. Understanding the role and value of your ideas is a key to commercialising them in an innovation economy. After all, how can you proceed without answering the question, 'what are your ideas worth?'

Action Steps

To assess your idea through valuation, start by asking yourself the following questions:

- How much do you believe your brand to be worth in the marketplace?
- What proportion of your business is 'plant and equipment' versus what can be considered as 'intangible assets'?
- How can you use the valuation approaches to assess the value of your idea?
- What do you believe is the most valuable intangible asset that you own?
- Intellectual property should be a yearly auditing process. How will you account for your brand this year?
- Download and complete the IP assessment from the last chapter. Ask yourself, 'how can I audit the assets?'
- Use the IP assessment valuation tool available at www.ipassist.com/au.

References

[i]Rumore, Martha M. 'Why You Should Care About Valuation of Intellectual Property.' https://www.frierlevitt.com/articles/why-you-should-care-about-valuation-of-intellectual-property/, (accessed August 1, 2021).

[ii] Ibid.

[iii] WIPO, 'Valuing Intellectual Property Assets.' https://www. wipo.int/sme/en/value_ip_assets/ , (accessed August 1, 2021).

[iv] Averkamp, Harold. 'What is Goodwill?" https://www.acc ountingcoach.com/blog/what-is-goodwill (accessed August 1, 2021).

[v] Fuhrmann, Ryan. 'The Titanic Proves Its Worth.' https://ww w.investopedia.com/financial-edge/0412/the-titanic-proves-its-worth.aspx (accessed August 1, 2021).

[vi] 'Titanic.' http://www.jamescamerononline.com/TitanicF AQ.htm (accessed August 1, 2021).

[vii] Atchison, Shane, '$26 billion and the incalculable value of LinkedIn.' *Vox.* https://www.vox.com/2016/6/15/11937240/ microsoft-linkedin-deal-economic-graph-professional-dat a, (accessed August 1, 2021).

[viii] Graham, Megan, 'Microsoft says LinkedIn topped $3 billion in revenue in the last year, outpacing Snap and Pinter-est.' https://www.cnbc.com/2021/04/27/microsoft-linkedin-topped-3-billion-in-ad-revenue-in-last-year.html#:~:text =Microsoft%20says%20LinkedIn%20topped%20%243,year %2C%20outpacing%20Snap%20and%20Pinterest&text=Mic rosoft%20said%20Tuesday%20that%20LinkedIn,in%20the, (accessed August 1, 2021).

[ix] Atwater, Peter. 'The Microsoft-LinkedIn Deal Proves We Overvalue Goodwill.' https://time.com/4376607/microsoft-lin kedin-goodwill/, (accessed August 1, 2021).

POINT 5: STRATEGISE AND COMMERCIALISE YOUR IDEA

'Ideas are easy. Implementing is hard.' –Guy Kawasaki

Adventurous men and women have for centuries sailed with ideas to solve problems all over the world. The difference today is that the internet is the sea, and our companies, the ships, must navigate this vast sea of opportunity to deliver our valuable ideas to the markets of today and tomorrow. As captain of your ship, you are the captain of your idea as well—an ideaologist. After building a boat and protecting your valuable cargo (your idea), you are ready to venture out into the world. Perhaps one of the hardest parts of the process for the captain is finding the quickest 'trade route' to the market.

Bringing a new idea to market is one of the most difficult and satisfying steps in sailing your idea towards success. It stands as one of the greatest challenges for every entrepreneur and innovation manager. Australia, for example, has to date an incredibly varied record in the commercialisation of their ideas. Some reach the market just in time, while others get lost at sea.

Building a trade route to your idea may be slow, but it is the goal behind a global commercialisation strategy. The route is often based on several pivoting strategies to ensure that an idea reaches its intended marketplace.

It is perfectly normal for a captain to draw up new routes or adjust old ones based on the new information they find along the way. This is the role of data in the modern world. We have access to new information like never before. As the commercialisation process is an arduous journey, you should prepare yourself to weather the storms that come your way during your commercialisation journey. By adopting a clear strategy during this final step, you can successfully sail towards the shores of commercial success.

How to start up smart

Although the protection and valuation of your new idea is crucial, it's equally important to explore opportunities for the commercialisation of your intellectual property. You can effectively reverse-engineer your commercial success by considering the different strategies available to you as you embark on your entrepreneurial journey. Your starting point is, and always, will be your vision. The strategies you use reflect who you are, what you want and what you stand for. By aligning your commercialisation strategy to your vision, you'll make sure your idea reaches its market and doesn't get lost at sea. Here are some important questions to ask at the outset:

- Do you envision being the owner of your business for years to come?

- Do you plan on exiting the business at any point? If so, when do you want to exit the business?
- Are you comfortable with giving equity investors some control over your business, or do you want to keep your idea close to you?

If you've watched the show *Shark Tank*, you know that much of the investment drama has to do with how much equity the founder is willing to give up. The drama stems from the fact that the founders have put little thought, if any at all, into their long-term vision for the future. If they did, they would be able to assess a deal almost immediately. Letting someone else invest in your business is a big decision, and it has long-term ramifications with financial consequences. While investment money may be a good short-term option, it may not necessarily be advantageous in the long run.

A commercialisation strategy, Jenny C. Servo writes, 'refers to the series of financing options that a company entertains to move its technology/product from concept to the marketplace.' As noted throughout this book, it is fundamental to ensure the idea and the heart of your identity is aligned in the pursuit of the commercialisation of any idea. This is your *true north*. Additionally, this will dictate and inform how you create a vital strategy around your next enterprise. However, your idea, no matter how well-thought and connected to your identity, needs a solid commercialisation strategy to see true success and make the impact you desire. This is when you must start thinking practically and strategically. What form will your idea take?

What do you need to make it a product or service ready to be delivered? Which distribution channels can you use? Who are your competitors, and what are their strategies?

This chapter will cover several commercialisation tactics that entrepreneurs have used successfully in leveraging the power of intellectual property over the years. It is always worth consulting intellectual property professionals and business strategists to map the best way forward. The seven key strategies for commercialisation are highlighted below:

1. Licensing your idea
2. Assigning your idea
3. Building strategic alliances
4. Handing equity on the idea
5. Creating spin-offs
6. Franchising your idea
7. Going Public—Initial Public Offering (IPO)

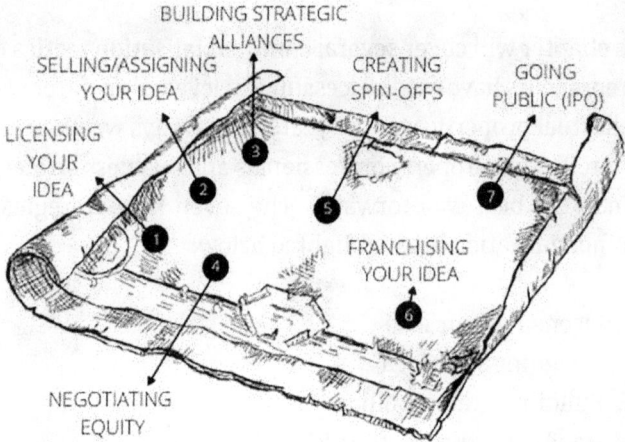

BUILDING STRATEGIC
ALLIANCES

SELLING/ASSIGNING
YOUR IDEA

CREATING
SPIN-OFFS

GOING
PUBLIC (IPO)

LICENSING
YOUR
IDEA

3

2

5

7

1

FRANCHISING
YOUR IDEA

4

6

NEGOTIATING
EQUITY

Strategy #1: Licensing your idea

Intellectual property rights do not exist in isolation. Their relationship is governed by contracts (and the chain of title), which define the legal rights of use of the intellectual property. The most common of these are known as licensing. The importance of licensing is often overlooked by fellow captains of ideas. Licensing is a tried-and-proved business model that can leverage your intellectual property for greater growth.

Licensing is one of the most ideal commercialisation strategies for many intellectual property owners. The greatest benefit of licensing your idea is that you retain ownership and can multiply the use of your intellectual property in markets all around the world. A licence effectively slices your intellectual property like a pie. Each slice of the pie may be served to several different customers/suppliers or retailers according to:

- Exclusivity
- Term
- Territory
- Duration
- Use
- Price

A licence grants licensees the right to use the intellectual property for a price and a defined set of terms and conditions. In some cases, you may have complete ownership of your idea while licensing it to others, thereby duplicating its value. I highly recommend considering a non-exclusive territory in the consideration of products and services. This is the most effective strategy to leverage the demand for your product or service. Here are some other questions to ask yourself in this process to get clear on how you can license your idea:

- What is the intellectual property being licensed?
- What is the nature of the intellectual property asset? Is it a patent, a trademark, a design or a copyright?
- What are the potential benefits licensing can bring to your idea?
- What is the considered valuation of the IP?
- Would it be more valuable to license to another individual

or marketplace?
- How will the intellectual property be used and who will use it? Will a right be used in a specific sector? Will the owner be able to license the IP to other sectors?
- What are the terms and conditions on which the IP is licensed and the payment structure?
- What is the duration of the licence? Are there termination clauses?
- What are the risks and how can they be mitigated?

Always remember that licensing grants others the right to use your intellectual property; it does not grant them ownership of the intellectual property. Ultimately, you remain the captain of your idea and your ship. You are in a position to dictate the terms of use through the licensing agreement. However, it is important to be deliberate and careful in choosing these licensing agreements. After all, they will determine the success of your licensing strategy.

Exclusive or non-exclusive licensing?

One of the most important considerations when assessing the terms of the idea is whether a term is either exclusive or non-exclusive. An exclusive licence grants exclusivity to a license holder, that is, the right to use the intellectual property in the Idea for their sole benefit to the exclusion of all others. An exclusive licence term attracts a premium price because it allows the licensee to generate more revenues from the intellectual property. A non-exclusive licence—the model most frequently used—grants the use of the idea to many licensees on a set of defined parameters as outlined above.

Rewards through royalties

The rewards for licensing your intellectual property are known as royalties. This is the financial benefit the intellectual property owner is entitled to for licensing or selling their ideas. It's important for captains of ideas to do their research. Ensuring an appropriate royalty rate is key to a successful commercial deal around your product, service or enterprise. Don't 'give away the farm' for the sake of the deal. For example, look at the licensing deals available for musicians, artists and writers. The royalty rate for these individuals can be draconian. Don't sign up to royalties that don't offer you a genuine reward.

When licensing your IP, there are several conditions and license royalties to consider. As IP Australia notes on its website, the intellectual property owner benefits from an exclusive licence by receiving 'an agreed sum that compensates for loss of future earnings and avoids the risk of the product not reaching the market or being successful.'[i] Meanwhile, the licensee benefits from an exclusive licence by making sure they will stay 'the sole recipient of the profits after bringing the product to a market-ready state.'[ii]

There is freedom that comes with structuring the financial terms of licences – that is, to share both the value of the licensed IP and the commercial risk of the licensed product between the licensor and the licensee. The financial terms in favour of the licensor can include:

- an initial upfront fixed fee
- annual fixed fees

- milestone payments to a licensor when the licensed product has achieved various stages of development or levels of sales
- periodic royalty payments
- reimbursement of the licensor's expenses under the licence
- and/or offsets against royalties for expenses of the licensee

It's important to check industry standards with respect to royalty rates locally and in overseas jurisdictions (if you market abroad). In the United States, for example, the Licensing Executive Society (LES) publishes information on the royalty rates for different industries. Do your own due diligence, engage with professionals and ask a lot of questions. This could avoid headaches and financial losses. Licensing is an important and valuable weapon. If the intellectual property is the bow, then licensing is the string. It can help win market share and, ultimately, build value for any enterprise. But the string can also break and hurt you, so make sure you use this weapon wisely.

Strategy #2: Sale or assignment of your idea

In contrast to licensing, assignment is the outright sale of your intellectual property. It involves transferring the ownership of your idea to another person for a set price. There are advantages and disadvantages to assigning your IP. On the one hand, IP assignment can be a viable strategy if receiving a large payment is preferable for your business. One the other hand, when assigning your IP, you cannot impose constraints on the new IP owner. When selling your IP, you need to consider what it cost you to research and develop the intellectual property, how much profit you want to make from the sale and the potential market value of the technology or IP. You can refer to the three valuation approaches to determine the value of your IP.

The purchaser may also want to pay royalties instead of a lump sum. When structuring payments in such a way, IP buyers make sure they are only paying if the intellectual property finds commercial success. You should pay close attention to the conditions of the assignment of intellectual property before adopting this strategy. Once your intellectual property is assigned, you have effectively sold the boat with your valuable cargo, flags and contracts. Establishing a fair remuneration for your idea is an important consideration when contemplating this strategy. The last thing you want to do is sell your intellectual property only to never reap the rewards. After all, your IP is your brainchild.

In my private practice, I always advise digital content businesses (e.g., photographers, website developers and filmmakers) to assign their project's IP rights to their clients. Because the client has paid you for your work, you can assign to them the copyright of the branding and marketing materials created on their behalf. This may be done by way of a drafted agreement or a set of terms and conditions. In contractual terms, it is known as 'consideration'. In this case, the 'consideration' is the price paid for a contract.

Strategy #3: Building strategic alliances

One of the most important and secure strategies you can use to advance your idea is partnerships. Partnerships enable ideas to gain traction quickly. Often, inventors approach international manufacturers with an idea and get discouraged because they don't even get advice. They feel they are locked out of the castle. The reality is that it may be dangerous for international manufacturers to be talking to you as they may already be working on a similar idea. Don't become despondent by this. Move on to the next potential strategic alliance.

Relationships are key in all businesses, and you can build strategic alliances that grow your idea like wildfire. The quickest road to market is to build powerful partnerships. Partnerships build credibility and trust; they can be a powerful way to enter the marketplace. Strategic partnerships can be anything from sharing contributions, ownership or control. Strategic partnerships, however, are not the same as joint ventures, which are more formal. The best partnerships are always those where partners augment each other's capacities and complement each other's skills, resulting in a product, service or offer that otherwise would not have been possible. In sum, a strategic partnership grants you access to new capabilities that allow you to become more competitive.

It's important to have contracts and written agreements for any partnership you create. These can be employment con-tracts, terms of agreement or fully fleshed-out partnership agreements. The effectiveness of these agreements lies not so much in the paper but in the process of communication that ensures trust and leads to the strategic goals. Remember that a good alliance is like a good marriage; it requires the respect and fair play characteristic of any good relationship. I recommend that participants do the following to develop successful collaborations:

- make a personal commitment to the partnership

- engage in the process of working with a lawyer to draft up an agreement, this builds mutual respect and trust
- take time to develop and maintain the relationship during this process
- clarify the relationship in a contractual form and then quickly put the contract away
- clarify mutual expectations and time frames
- maintain an awareness of the partner's problems
- learn to interpret particular responses in a culturally appropriate way
- recognise a partner's independence
- celebrate success together

Strategy #4: Negotiating equity

Equity negotiations are typical in intellectual property commercialisation. It is very common for founders to hand equity (shares) of their business in exchange for an investment, and sometimes guidance. That is what happens in the show *Shark Tanks.* Typically, the entrepreneurs who participate in the show need more capital than they currently have. The lack of capital may be preventing them from sailing in the right direction or at the speed they desire. Hence, they are seeking investments from savvy and experienced investors—the "sharks"—looking for a good business opportunity. While getting investments is great, it is important to consider the long-term consequences of such agreements. At the end of the day, the question will be about ownership? Who owns the boat? Who has the most shares and therefore the most control?

When negotiating equity in your business, it's crucial to record your conversations and be clear around equity. These negotiations will challenge issues of power and trust. Therefore, clarity is key. Deepak Malhota, in a *Harvard Business Review* article, notes a few key elements to ensure that your reward is appropriate when negotiating equity in your idea.

Understand your leverage. As Malhota notes, you can utilize your alternatives to the deal to create leverage in your negotiation. If you have other valuable alternatives to achieve your outcomes, then you are not in a position of dependency to the deal. Without negotiating in bad faith, you can demonstrate your detachment to the deal by using your alternative routes.

Focus on value, not just valuation. A founder-investor relationship is more than numbers and bottom-line. Control and value of the company is just as important as valuation. Investors think big picture, and they can tell when a founder makes rookie mistakes such as sacrificing control for a higher valuation. Make sure you think big picture and think about the value, not just the valuation, of the business.

Maximize trust. Beyond financial projections, investors want to determine who they associate with. The relationship will be a long-lasting one, so it's important for them to feel secure. If you find the investor in a vulnerable situation, use the opportunity to build trust rather than to take advantage of it. Such trust will go a long way and will make your relationship more profitable in the future.

Strive for understanding. Seek to understand the potential investor and his goals. Be prepared to educate him or her about why exercising too much power could hurt *both* parties in the long term. Even though you have financial incentives, you should see the investor as an ally with whom you create a fair collaboration.[iii]

When considering handing equity to an investor, remember that you are building a relationship that affects the control and the direction of the business and that more than money is at stake. Don't make the mistake of rushing into an investment deal because you need capital. Deals must be carefully considered because they have long-term consequences on the company, its founders and its team.

Strategy #5: Creating a spin-off company

A spin-off is a separate company established to bring a technology developed by a parent company to the market. A conventional spin-off company can be set up in two ways: it can be a new, separate company or one created from a parent organisation that contributes financial, human and intellectual capital. The aim of a spin-off is to further develop and commercialise the IP created at, and assigned by, the parent organisation. Along with the relevant intangible asset, the parent organisation transfers the obligations and risks of commercialising the IP.

According to IP Australia, 'a start-up can also be a company established independently of the existence of any parent organisation, with a view to exploiting the licensed intangible asset. This encourages interested venture capitalists to invest in the development of the IP created by the organisation.'[iv] Spin-off companies are generally created because the owners can use them to focus on certain products or services, attract venture capital and increase returns. Think of it as building a second ship that holds a different cargo from yours and may be headed in a different direction. That second, more focused ship may be more attractive to investors because it is not encumbered with other products or services that may be less lucrative.

When considering creating a spin-off company, consider the time, financial capital and human capital required to make it happen. While it can be lucrative, it can also be long, costly and tedious. Make sure your original company already does well and you have the necessary resources to invest in a spin-off. Creating a spin-off company is an advanced commercialisation strategy and should be used by entrepreneurs with at least some experience. It's preferable to consult with professionals and do your due diligence before moving forward with such a strategy.

Strategy #6: Franchising

Once your business reaches a certain level of success, you may want to further expand your business activities. However, you may not want to do so by borrowing capital. In that case, you can consider franchising your business, which consists of licensing your intellectual property for other people to use in exchange for a set price. Simply described, franchising is licensing on steroids. It effectively creates a system wherein people, the franchisees, rent your name and reputation and operate independently. According to IP Australia, the factors that typically characterise a franchise relationship include:

- **licensing IP**: in return for an agreed payment, the franchisee is allowed to use the franchisor's IP rights

- **an ongoing relationship**: the relationship involves multiple sales of the franchised product or service, with the franchisor giving continuous assistance to the franchisee in establishing, maintaining and promoting the franchise
- t**he manner of operating**: the franchisee agrees to follow instructions for operating the franchise as set by the franchisor, which could include quality control and territorial restrictions.[v]

IP Australia also notes several aspects to take into account when franchising:

- franchising is a method or system for distributing goods and services
- the franchisor owns the IP rights over the marketing system, service method or special product
- the franchisee pays for the right to trade under the brand name
- the franchisee benefits from coordinated marketing efforts and a developed business system.[vi]

Before considering a commercialisation strategy such as franchising, it's important to make sure your intellectual property is properly protected and valued. This way, both your interests and the interest of potential franchisees are protected. For the franchiser, it's important to preserve the value of the intellectual property; for the franchisee, it's crucial to have an effective business that runs based on the franchisor's intellectual property.

There are different types of relationships built around franchising. IP Australia notes the following ones:

- **Manufacturer-Retailer**: Where the retailer (as the franchisee) sells the franchisor's product directly to the public. Motor vehicle dealerships are a good example of a manufacturer-retailer relationship.
- **Manufacturer-Wholesaler**: Where the franchisee under licence manufactures and distributes the franchisor's product. A good example of a manufacturer-wholesaler relationship is soft drink bottling arrangements such as Amtell.
- **Wholesaler-Retailer**: Where the retailer (as a franchisee) purchases products for retail sale from a franchisor wholesaler. A good example would be a hardware store such as Bunnings or Chemist Warehouse.[vii]

Franchising is one of the most leveraged forms of intellectual property. Success stories abound, but so too failures. The franchising process is highly complex and can be a massive undertaking for any new captain. Franchising should be carefully considered with legal advice. That said, the Australian Competition and Consumer Commission provides a free franchisee's manual on its website. This document can help you make sense of the different requirements as well as whether it is the right strategy for you.

Strategy #7: Going public with an initial public offering

Every business starts off privately owned. When you incorporate your business with your local government, you register the business owners, whether you're on your own or have business partners. From that point on, you own shares of the business. However, once the business has become valuable, you may choose to go public and to sell shares of your business to the public. In today's world, going public is glamorous and the ultimate goal of many businesses (especially in the technology industry). Going public is a means to raise capital purely through the valuation of the business (which makes it all the more important to properly value the business, as outlined in 'Accelerate'). Once on the stock market, the shares of a business represent the value of the business. They go up and down based on the perceived value of the business.

It's important that the perceived value of a business is not the same as the actual value. For example, Amazon CEO Jeff Bezos rightly points out that the 'stock is not the company' in an interview with Bloomberg Markets and Finance. He recounts how, because of the internet bubble, the Amazon stock went from US$113 to US$6 while every internal business metric was getting better and fast.[viii] In other words, the perceived value of Amazon was low, but its real value was high and increasing. Such instances provide savvy investors with the opportunity to buy stocks for a low price and see their shares grow in value.

Although the initial public offering (IPO) is great to raise capital and put your business on the map, it's also a long and costly method strategy. It requires an enormous amount of legal, accounting, marketing, public relation and managerial work. Moreover, once publicly owned, the company must have a board of directors and be fully transparent with its shareholders. Before you consider going public, there are other financing options you can consider:

First-round financing methods include:

- Families, friends and fools
- Sweat equity and owner's equity
- R&D partnerships
- Seed financing from venture capitalists and angels
- Equity investment from a private investor or angel network

Second-round financing methods include:

- A private placement
- A line of credit from a bank
- Profits invested back into the company

Ultimately, the initial public offering (IPO) is a powerful and glorious strategy, but it is also risky and complex. Entrepreneurs must be mindful about using this strategy at the right time and to take the necessary steps before using it. Positioning an idea in the market is a lucrative, fulfilling endeavour, but it requires considerable amounts of time and financial planning.

Case study: Atlassian

A great success story that demonstrates the power of an initial public offering is Australian-founded Atlassian. Founded in 2010 off a credit card, the tech giant floated on the Nasdaq stock exchange, closing the day with a market value of US$5.8 billion (AU$8 billion) only five years later only. The public valuation was well above its 2014 private valuation of US$3.3 billion (AU$4.5 billion). Atlassian's public valuation made it the most successful listing of an Australian company in the U.S. Atlassian has also catapulted its two founders straight into the top 20 of the BRW Rich List.

Mike Cannon-Brookes and Scott Farquhar were both 22 years old and studying at the University of New South Wales when they founded Atlassian, which now employs over 5,000 people as of 2021. Today it serves international clients including Twitter, Verizon and the US space agency NASA, which uses Atlassian technology on its Space Rover. In 2015, despite his successes, Farquhar said Atlassian was still focused on innovation and creating a long-term company that solves fundamental problems. The valuation of Atlassian demonstrates the enormous value this journey has created in intellectual property and through an IPO. As of August 2021, Atlassian is worth US$47.1 billion.

Action Steps

Ask yourself the following questions to determine the commercialisation strategies you should use to bring your idea to market:

- Do you want to sell your idea or share the equity for far greater growth?
- What proportion of the business are you committed to selling or sharing for the growth of your enterprise? What percentage of equity are you willing to give up?
- Consider what licensed intellectual property you have to commercialise. List it on the IP assessment workshop available at www.ipassist.com.au.
- Consider both exclusive and non-exclusive licences. Which would give you the most leverage?
- As an existing business or organisation what financial positive function of your business could be a spin-off company?
- As an existing business or organisation, what product or service could be a licensed system that could create a franchise?
- Consider the road to the initial public offering (IPO). What are the steps necessary to reach this goal? You can work on your commercialisation strategy back from there.
- Have you protected your intellectual property in preparation for third-party investment?

References

[i] IP Australia, 'Types of Licences.' https://www.ipaustralia.gov.au/understanding-ip/commercialise-your-ip/types-licences (accessed August 1, 2021).

[ii] Ibid.

[iii] Malhota, Deepak. 'How to Negotiate with VCs.' https://hbr

.org/2013/05/how-to-negotiate-with-vcs (accessed August 1, 2021).

[iv] IP Australia. 'Choose your commercialisation vehicle option.' https://www.ipaustralia.gov.au/understanding-ip/commercialise-your-ip/choose-your-commercialisation-vehicle-option (accessed August 1, 2021).

[v] IP Australia. 'Franchising and IP.' https://www.ipaustralia.gov.au/understanding-ip/commercialise-your-ip/franchising-and-ip (accessed August 1, 2021).

[vi] Ibid.

[vii] Ibid.

[viii] Bloomberg Markets and Finance. 'Jeff Bezos Says Amazon Is 'Not the Company.' https://www.youtube.com/watch?v=msFwJ5xpg_g (accessed August 1, 2021).

Conclusion

'Don't ask what you want when you grow up, but ask want problems do you want to solve'—Jaime Casap, Google

U p until recently, I lived in Melbourne, Australia, where I wrote much of this book. Out the front of my home was an old, dilapidated shed, which once was the distribution centre for the Brunswick Brickworks. The corrugated iron is an ochre red decaying in the face of modernity. Pigeons now make it their home and flutter freely amongst its aching architecture. Once a thriving factory, the Brunswick Brickworks used to employ nearly 10,000 migrants. With such manpower, it produced enough bricks to build more than half of Melbourne's surrounding suburbs.

The Brunswick Brickworks was instrumental not only in introducing new technology into the Australian construction industry, but also in restructuring the commercial landscape, leading to takeovers and mergers. Moreover, it played a role in the creation of brick cartels that set the price and production quotas for competing brick companies. When I walked through its old steel and wood structure, I often thought about how the wheels of change have churned the commercial landscape in which it was created. We now sit above these ancient factories and focus on blue limitless horizons that lie beyond. 'The shed' is now a relic of the old industrial revolution.

Today I am doing business in the last Australian frontier, Darwin, Northern Territory. I cannot help but contemplate how far my own journey has taken me, how far we have come as a nation and how instrumental entrepreneurs and thought leaders were in the vast progress we've witnessed in the past few hundred years. Take the vast distance between Adelaide and Darwin, for example; it tells a story of technology and of two founders history remembers differently, John McDouall Stuart and Sir Charles Todd. This story is an inspiring one, but it's also a cautionary tale about intellectual property and commercialisation.

Between the ages of 43 and 53, John McDouall Stuart, also known as the 'Explorer's Explorer', made six expeditions to conquer the final frontier and discover the heart of Australia. The roads he travelled came to be known as 'Mr. Stuart's Track'. It's almost unimaginable how Stuart, riding atop a horse named Polly, traversed these vast landscapes, slowly moving 50 km per day, with only 4 weeks rations to hold him until finding his way to the end. It took him six attempts, but he finally made it to the wild tropics of the north. Stuart discovered much intellectual property along the way, enshrined in his detailed diaries of map routes, bush foods and indigenous survival tips. Most importantly, his knowledge allowed colonials to move to these territories.

Every time Stuart returned from his trip, he was visited by a government official or other notable entrepreneur to whom he gave his ideas, often bedridden and suffering from scurvy. John McDouall Stuart survived it all (unlike other explorers, who perished upon returning to Melbourne). However, Stuart died a pauper back home in Scotland, and only seven people attended his funeral. After his death, only history noted his achievements and gave him the recognition he richly deserved. Towns, highways and monuments were named after him, but he tasted neither riches nor fame during his lifetime. He never protected his intellectual property.

Stuart's life is a cautionary tale: to be the first to market does not mean you will be enriched by your ideas. Intellectual property counts. Commercialisation counts. In fact, they count more than anything else. Steve Jobs' genius lay in the creation of IP and in commercialisation; he didn't have Steve Wozniak's technical abilities. Still, Jobs is Apple's face to this day, even years after his passing.

The unfortunate reality is that Stuart gave away his intellectual property and people were as glad to take it as much as he was to share it. He had brilliant strategies to conquer the North, but not one to benefit from his ideas. Sir Charles Todd, however, had a very different story. Only two years after Stuart had found the North, Todd set the visionary goal to connect Adelaide and Darwin. He embarked on the journey to connect the two cities with the newest technology available then: the telegraph line.

Back then, Adelaide and Melbourne were a long way down from the rest of the world, and Todd recognised the importance of connecting the Southern land with the mother country and with

Europe and Asia for the development of our young country. Even though Todd did not create the telegraph line, he did have a remarkable strategy to connect the North.

And with Stuart's plans in hand, he did.

Mobilising 30,000 men from Adelaide, in the South, to Darwin, in the North, the funded project managed to connect through twelve telegraph repeater stations, with the official line connecting in Daly Waters not far from the first international air hanger in the Northern Territory. Todd succeeded in connecting places with technology, an achievement he managed in just two years.

The age of digital business and cloud computing are bringing a silver lining for those who have the courage to create the world of tomorrow. Seventy percent of students are currently studying for careers that will no longer exist in the next 15 years. The students who will create the future of tomorrow should be asked not what they want to be when they grow up, but rather what problem they seek to solve. But how does our generation prepare for the changes ahead, caught between two great industrial revolutions?

'The next frontiers are those of the mind,' Winston Churchill once said. Those seeking a job will be replaced by those seeking opportunities. The innovation age welcomes an economy based on ideas that solve problems. And they are fuelled by the combustion steam engine of ideas. Those with the ability to recognise their ideas as intellectual property and take the sure and steady path to market will be in a greatly advantageous position to build long-lasting enterprises.

Every industrial revolution spurs considerable advancements in health, education and technology. It also produces more wealth than was available to previous generations. These changes happen whether we desire them or not. It's important to avoid being a Luddite and get left behind; it is much better to embrace technological changes, especially today. We have no excuse. Never in human history has it been easier to pursue the fruit of our ideas. The Ideaology compass outlined in this book shows you how you can begin to create this future. What you've seen in this book is only the tip of the iceberg. The Ideas Economy hides much more wealth and secrets than I can write about in a short book like this.

New frontiers do exist, and they are born in the students of today, who create the future of tomorrow. In the 14th century, you may have hoped to become a sailor on one of the impressive sailing ships to find treasures. Many died on those arduous voyages. Today, however, the risk of starting a venture based on your ideas is born in those that have the courage to take the adventure. And there is no death, no true failures—just a journey rich with adventure.

The best compass you have is your identity and, like the pearl diver brothers who saw the opportunity in becoming the captains of their own ship, you too have the opportunity to be the captain of your idea. This is the premise of Ideaology. During your adventure, you will explore new blue oceans and endure rough seas. You will also likely go off course, and you'll have to navigate towards safe harbours once more. As a captain, you will make new friends, allies and enemies all along the way.

You may also get marooned and experience a dark night of the soul. You may even wish to quit and sail back to the familiar harbours of home. You will be required to navigate uncharted waters of your own identity. Still, the adventure of your ventures will be rewarding and memorable journey of your life. The search for your treasure is what counts. Your ideas can create intellectual property used by millions around the world.

But don't take my word for it just yet. This journey is yours. Whether you succeed or fail by you own measures may become irrelevant. That you had the courage to go on the quest—this is what truly counts. And in your search for new frontiers, you will come to understand your ideas are worth gold.

Let's continue the conversation

The technological advancements we've seen are only the beginning of the Ideas Economy. To ensure that the future remains inspiring for you, I have launched a weekly video blog series named *Finding Gold*, which will explore the best and brightest ideas from Australian and foreign entrepreneurs. Be sure to enter your details for upcoming posts at www.garethbenson.com.

Free gift: idea assessment tool

I've created a free, downloadable 10-point questionnaire that will help you evaluate your latest idea and opportunity. This assessment is an invaluable tool I have developed over many years and will provide an indication of your identity in relation to your idea, and the intellectual property that may lie within it. This can provide you with a springboard to a discussion about how to leverage your most valuable asset: your idea. To get a free copy, go to www.ipassist.com.au.

Intellectual property workshop/self-assessment

I have prepared a three-hour workshop and e-learning program called *IDEAOLOGY: Your Compass to Your Intellectual Property in an Innovation Economy.* This e-learning program takes the concepts discussed in this book and demonstrates them to you via a number of videos on how to actually leverage your idea.

IP Assist Masterclass

I also have a custom-tailored masterclass that offers insights into specific intellectual property topics endorsed by IP Australia and presented by myself and other qualified intellectual property lawyers. We have offered this masterclass at the Darwin Innovation Hub, Entourage, RMIT University and Referall Hub, Melbourne. For more information, visit www.ipassist.com.au.

Turn on your bright ideas!

Now it's your turn to hit me with your bright ideas. If you take a photo of yourself reading my book with a thoughtful gesture and upload it to Instagram and tag @garethspeaks. I will send you a coupon code to receive 50% off my *Understanding IP* Workshop.

Strategy consulting

If you are interested in consulting with respect to the commercialisation of your venture, let's discuss how to leverage your organisation's intellectual property through a commercialization IP strategy. Further information can be obtained at www.garethbenson.com

Keynote presentation

Lastly, if you think that your business or customers would be inspired by the innovation of *IDEAOLOGY*, please be sure to let me know. I'm regularly seeing clients both domestically and internationally and would only be too happy to speak at your next conference on how businesses can benefit from the 'Idea Boom'.

I sincerely hope you have enjoyed reading *IDEAOLOGY* and, just as importantly, are inspired to engage in innovation yourself. I truly would love to speak about your bright idea and your story.

Further resources

Over the past 5 years, I have interviewed notable Australian entrepreneurs on the value of their idea. I have listed these on my website for further commentary and discussion as they apply to your business. Visit **www.garethbenson.com.**

ACKNOWLEDGEMENT

First, I must thank the idea makers and creators who have informed the safe passage of this book. It is your adventures and misadventures that have also guided my own journey in entrepreneurship.

I acknowledge Kylie Bartlet, my first book mentor, and emerging entrepreneur Léandre Larouche from Canada, who has demonstrated you can learn from anyone on their digital entrepreneurship journey.

I also would like to acknowledge my mother Robyn Benson, who worked tirelessly as an academic at Monash University to put four kids through school, along with my father, who assisted with the first chapter of the edits of *IDEAOLOGY* five years ago.

I also acknowledge those who have provided feedback and support along the journey: Hafize Toker and Lauren Riley, who identified the heroic currency in me; John Perry, who offered valued support over the years; Mitchell Harold, Dr Maurice Roussety and Sandra Spencer, who assisted with the launch of *IDEAOLOGY*.

Finally, another heartfelt thank you to the idea makers, creators and history shakers that have inspired us all. Thank you for your thoughts.

About the Author

GARETH BENSON, LLB is a commercial and intellectual property lawyer who has been practising in Australia for over twenty years. He is the principal of IP ASSIST Gareth Benson Lawyers & Associates. Gareth has worked on major intellectual property deals including blockbuster movies and some of the world's most valuable brands. He has also operated as a digital entrepreneur in the Ideas Economy for over 10 years. He currently resides in Darwin, Australia.

You can connect with me on:

🌐 https://www.garethbenson.com